Bird People

Bird People

A MEMOIR

Letitia L. Moffitt

CANTRAIP
PRESS

CHARLESTON, ILLINOIS

Cantraip Press
2317 Saratoga Place
Charleston, IL 61920
www.cantraip.com

Book Layout ©2017 BookDesignTemplates.com

Cover Image by Laura Anne Welle

Cover Design by Damonza

Ordering Information:
Quantity sales. Special discounts are available on quantity purchases by corporations, associations, and others. For details, contact the "Special Sales Department" at the address above.

Bird People/ Letitia L. Moffitt. -- 1st ed.
ISBN 978-1-9427371-8-6

Library of Congress Control Number: 2019934170

Contents

Acknowledgments

THANK YOU, MARY MADDOX, for being my publisher, a great friend, and one of my all-time favorite writers. I can't believe how lucky I am to know you.

Thanks to Melissa Ames, Megan Holt, Jennifer Hrejsa-Hudson, Anna-Elise Price, and Cynthia Boatright Raleigh for providing helpful comments on drafts of this book.

Thank you, Laura Anne Welle, for the beautiful cover image as well as many of the great photos within the book. And thanks to Laura, Theresa, and Julia Welle for letting me be part of your family and giving me hope for the future (no small feat given how pessimistic I can be).

Nothing I achieve would be possible without three people who have been there for me my entire life: Leonard, Shan-Ying, and Laura Moffitt.

Ken Welle, my life is so much better with you in it. Let's run together forever, OK? (We'll bring snacks.)

And finally, to Boston, Phoenix, and Fred: Love? Love.

CHAPTER 1

How We Met

MET HIS DOG BEFORE I met him.

There's a five-mile trail about ten minutes from town where my trail-running group, The Buffalo, meets each Thursday evening. It isn't the most interesting or challenging trail in the world, but this is east-central Illinois, where varied topography is hard to come by, and for runners who prefer dirt to pavement, we're lucky to get even this. That particular day I was running with a friend, Kathy, and at some point in the early miles I became aware that a friendly, mid-size dog was bounding alongside us.

Body language can reveal all sorts of things, even when the body is four-legged and furry, and I figured out pretty quickly that the dog was not Kathy's. Something about the mutt's movements suggested more *you seem like good people, so I will run with you—isn't this fun?* than *Kathy Kathy Kathy, run with Kathy, chase down rabbit to bring to Kathy, what's Kathy doing? Oh, she's running! Run with Kathy!* She was clearly *someone's* dog, though, with a well-groomed, frosty red coat and a tame demeanor, so I asked.

Kathy glanced down. "Oh, that's Cayenne." Almost as an afterthought, she added, "She's with Ken."

That seemed to be all the explanation required, so I guessed Cayenne did this regularly, went happily gamboling off with strangers. *I don't know who this Ken person is,* I remember thinking, faintly disapproving, *but he has a nice dog.*

When we finished our run, Ken-person was not there. "He went back out to look for Cayenne," one of The Buffalo told us.

Well for goodness sake. I looked down at the happy red mutt. Now what were we supposed to do? Go looking for him and keep chasing each other in circles until one of us collapsed? Despite the fact that everyone knew Cayenne, nobody had Ken's phone number, so we couldn't call him to come back to the parking lot. It was getting late and we couldn't very well leave until they were reunited, but nobody else seemed terribly concerned.

Ken-person finally returned. "There you are, you knucklehead," he said affectionately, and Cayenne, overjoyed, looked up with shining eyes. *Why yes, I am a knucklehead! Thank you for saying so!*

He was tall, with the build of someone who looked more like he'd been a football player and not a runner in his youth, he had a nice smile, and he looked vaguely familiar. Only later, driving home, I realized he must have been a long-standing member of The Buffalo given how everyone seemed to know him, or at least his dog. Yet he had made very little impression on me until then. He was quiet, he was a fast runner (he'd probably finished the five-mile course a good ten minutes ahead of Kathy and me), and he liked to let his dog run free. Beyond that I knew nothing.

That's not unusual with the trail runners I've met. One of the things I liked about this group was that we rarely talked about our personal lives. You could run with someone for months and have no clue what they did for a living—and not feel any particular need to know. So much of the time, we present ourselves to others through how we look and what we say. On the trail, there's none of that; there's just what we *do*, what all of us are doing at that moment together. Even though I doubt there are many other species that run around in circles for the hell of it, I like to think we're more like our animal selves when we run in the woods, living solely in the here and now.

The funny thing is I used to *hate* trail running, wasn't a runner at all, in fact, for most of my life. I started when I was 37 years old, having just moved from New York City to a small college town in rural Illinois. It was not the first time I had radically redefined myself—I was born and raised in semi-rural Hawaii, far removed from either the East Village of Manhattan or the cornfields of the Heartland—and it would not be the last. Barely a month into my new life, a friend at work told me about a 5K that benefited the local public library. Rural Illinois was *flat*, I reasoned. How hard could running be? Very, as it turned out, yet something happened to me after that first painfully slow ordeal besides gorging on the pancake breakfast provided for the runners, thus ensuring I consumed far more calories than I had burned: I vowed that I would get fit. As God was my witness, I would *earn* those pancakes. And then I would have seconds.

From there, somehow I went from barely making it around the block without collapsing to regularly taking on marathons and even ultramarathons—that is, distances beyond 26.2 miles, which I had not even known existed in my previous life except by car. It's not unusual to hear stories of people discovering running later in life; it's exercise a person can do on their own, after all, with relatively little expense or preparation—and, most of all, no humiliating sessions with baffling equipment, surrounded by the young and the chiseled, in a mirrored room where you can't delude yourself about your lack of strength, coordination, and flexibility.

But after a while I wasn't doing it to be healthy. After a while it *wasn't* all that healthy. I'm not an MD but I still know that black toenails probably aren't a good thing. I kept doing it because I loved it. There is solitude and peace. There is rigorous challenge and then rapturous reward for getting through the rigorous challenge. There's a high—for me, a slow, steady one, not a crazy crash-and-burn adrenaline rush but something that feels deeper and more en-during. And yes, there's pain. Lots of it. After long runs I hurt in ways I never thought possible. I once chipped a tooth during a run. I strained muscles I couldn't pronounce. The thing about that, though: the suffering you take on voluntarily is very different from the one you are helpless to prevent. In truth, nothing too terrible has happened to me running, nothing I couldn't chuckle about later, and many good things have happened. I got reasonably fit for the first time in my life. I made friends with a lot of like-minded lunatics who run crazy distances for fun. And as I said, I met a certain dog and her person.

Near the end of *Pride and Prejudice*, Elizabeth Bennet jokes that she first became attracted to Mr. Darcy when she saw his palatial estate. She's mostly joking—but not completely. She's not a gold-digger, but she was still *awfully* impressed with that mansion. Likewise (sort of), the moment I became interested in Ken as more than just another Buffalo runner was when I discovered he was recently divorced. (Later on he would tell me he'd been interested in *me* from the start but hadn't known whether I was available either.) I was not desperate for a partner. I liked my independence. But I also liked companionship, sex, and the possibility of not being alone forever—plus, at my age, the population of datable men was limited. I decided it made sense to get to know him better. This probably does not sound like the beginning of an epic love along the lines of a Jane Austen novel, but that's fine with me. Even epic love needs to be pragmatic sometimes— just ask Elizabeth Bennet.

I quickly learned that the initial impression I'd gotten of him—quiet, good runner, loves his dog— made up some of the key aspects of his character. Quiet, I liked. One of my favorite things about running is you don't have to talk. You *can't* talk a lot of the time, if you're running with someone faster than you, which I was with him. It was a mixed blessing. Running with faster runners has helped me get faster myself. It has also made me feel very close to death. Not ideal for getting to know someone. I discovered there were a select few topics that could get him chatting, and because it was a struggle for me to keep up with even his relaxed pace, I seized upon these topics so that I could breathe while he talked. He loved his three daughters and would happily describe their accomplishments. He was a veterinarian at our town's university vet clinic and enjoyed his job. And he was a hard-core runner who had qualified for the Boston Marathon three times. "What are their ages and interests?" "What kinds of animals do you treat at the clinic and what's your favorite?" "What was it like to run Boston?" I would blurt and hope he had some lengthy stories to accompany his answers. Often he did, his stories interrupted every now and then with a yell of *"CAYENNE!"* when we hadn't seen the old girl in a while because she'd spotted a fun-looking pond a mile back or caught a whiff of some interesting poop.

The dog was another happy topic for conversation. I learned that Cayenne was a shelter dog, her exact day of birth unknown, so Ken had decided to attribute it to March 17, St. Patrick's Day, for ease of remembrance. She probably didn't have any Irish breed in her, though she was a redhead—red-eared, in any case, the rest of her a mix of red frosted with white. She was nearly 12 when I met her and her muzzle was completely white with age, yet she was still most definitely a distance runner's dog, putting in double-digit mileage and making it look easy. "You should have seen her in her prime," he told me. "She had distance *and* speed. You wouldn't believe how fast she could go. She might cover the distance between here and that tree," and he pointed far across the prairie, "in seconds. And still run another ten miles after that!"

I liked hearing him talk about Cayenne, and I liked running with her, but I had mixed feelings about this as well. To put it bluntly, dogs are pretty much never supposed to be off-leash in public. Trifling legalities seldom concerned The Buffalo; at the park where we ran trails on Thursdays, dogs weren't supposed run off leash, alcohol wasn't supposed to be consumed, and people were supposed to leave after sunset, but *eh, shrug* seemed to be the general attitude about all that. Ken didn't drink and he seldom lingered after he finished running, but Cayenne went off-leash as soon as we entered the woods. Granted, The Buffalo seldom ran into any other people during Thursday runs, and even on weekends the trails were never crowded, but there were occasionally other runners or walkers, and an unleashed dog was a danger. In Cayenne's case I could see that she was more likely to run in front of you and trip you than jump on you or bite you, but that was irrelevant. People always think their dogs are good around people until they aren't. I daresay this had been the case with the French woman who famously received a face transplant after her dog— a golden retriever, of all things, the poster-dog of good-natured sweetness—chewed hers off in the middle of the night. Even if nothing that dramatic ever happened, there was still the minor drama of having to backtrack and search the trails for Cayenne, only to discover that she'd returned to the parking lot on her own and was waiting patiently by Ken's car for water and ear scratches. The next week it would be exactly the same.

Again and again, I wondered: Why did he keep letting Cayenne off leash? But I already knew the answer to that. I'd known it before I'd met them, ever since I finished that terrible 5K and didn't stop there.

Cayenne loved to run, *loved* it. On a leash, she got exercise; off leash, on her own, she experienced pure joy. Even as the most domesticated of animals—the first, in fact, bred 30,000 years ago to run alongside hunters—a dog is still a force of nature, a life, moving on her own through the world. If Cayenne were merely a pet, she would have simply followed us on the trail, but of course she didn't do that. As soon as the leash was off she went bounding away on her own, excited by smells and sounds, red ears flapping like butterfly wings, so light and full of life.

And yet each time, she came back. This was trail running, for her and for us: a moment of wildness, and a return to what was familiar and comforting.

Why am I beginning a book about birds with a running dog? I'm not an ornithologist; I am someone who ended up inadvertently caring for various pets, including a dog and, later, some macaws. At the point when I met Ken and Cayenne, I was looking for life to be simpler. It had not been for me up until then; it had been complicated and messy—pointlessly so, I felt as I moved firmly into middle-age. I had had my youthful moments of wildness; now I wanted to find the familiar and the comforting. If I ultimately found love, I wanted it to be, if not simple, since that was rarely possible, at least free of needless drama. I loved running, because what I got out of it was greater than what it cost me. Later, I began to love a man, and his dog, because we enjoyed the same things, we didn't make too many demands on each other, and we could take care of those demands with relative ease. I loved these things even while I understood that none of us was without faults, flaws, and complications. Yet there are some complications—among them, the kind that comes cloaked in pretty feathers—it would seem you can't ever be sufficiently prepared for.

CHAPTER 2

How I Passed the First Test

EARLY IN OUR RELATIONSHIP when I told people my new boyfriend was a veterinarian, they frequently had the same reaction: a quick "oh!" and a smile of delight. It wasn't the impressed "oh!" I'd have gotten if I'd said he was a surgeon, nor the pause followed by a polite but flat "oh" that might follow, say, "dentist." When you say veterinarian, people are relieved; surely a person who cares for animals for a living must be kind and decent. Even people who don't have pets or don't particularly like animals tend to think so, and the ones that do love animals become positively aglow. And they aren't wrong; there's a lot of truth, I think, to the image we have of animal doctors. They almost always go into this profession out of love for all creatures great and small. After all, they go through as much schooling as people-MDs—and come out with just as massive a debt—while making a fraction of the salary. There are those few people who like to accuse vets of price gouging, of charging inflated fees for services that they should be doing out of the goodness of their hearts, or something, which is one of the unfortunate aspects of a profession with a kind-and-caring image. But in general everyone I told this information to was pleased.

I was pleased for many of the same reasons, but also because it meant that animals were back in my life.

My sister and I, when we were kids: *We want a dog!* Our parents, over and over: *You say you want a dog but do you know how to care for a dog do you know how to be responsible for a dog and just who's going to feed the dog who's going to walk the dog who's going to clean up the dog's poop.* We listened with impatiently nodding heads, waiting for a pause so that we could promise to pick up every piece of poop that ever issued forth from our pup's behind with such alacrity that people would wonder whether the dog ever took a dump at all. I usually left these assurances up to my sister, the responsible one, the one who couldn't leave our room without making sure all the books on the shelf were aligned and all the clothes in the closet were spaced equidistantly, no errant sleeve rumpled. Privately I snickered at her fussiness, but in public—or at least the public of our parents when they were hearing our pleas for pets—I pretended I was as much of a neat freak as she was.

This strategy paid off. Over the years we got rabbits, guinea pigs, two dogs, lots of fish, and a bird, a Javanese finch, who would lay eggs at the bottom of her cage and then kick them from one end to the other like soccer balls. That was childhood, though; when I met Ken, I hadn't had a pet in nearly 30 years. In fact, I had hardly shared my life with anyone or anything during that time. I wanted pets as a child because I was lonely; as an adult I was still lonely, but I discovered that independence meant more to me than companionship. There had been one serious boyfriend, back in New York, who made it excruciatingly clear early in our relationship that he thought marriage was a bad idea, and that even living together, given that his apartment was small and mine was pretty much a walk-in closet, was less than desirable. I shrugged and played along for several years.

As I began dating again later in life, I had to face the fact that the majority of men my age had children. The prospect of stepchildren was terrifying, a certain lose-lose: responsibility for the well-being of someone who had every reason to resent my presence in their life. The evil of the fairy tale stepmother has long been established. She's a vain, selfish gold-digger, and those are her *good* qualities; she's also cruel, tyrannical, and devoid of maternal instincts. She eats men for breakfast, children for lunch, and cute baby animals for dinner, often posting pictures of her cringing, terrified meals right before they are devoured alive. Or at least that's how I imagined any potential step-progeny seeing me. Ken's three daughters were not really children by the time I entered their lives; the youngest was already 16 and the other two had graduated from high school and moved on into adulthood. What's more, they made it blessedly easy on me. The oldest in particular had grasped the fact that their parents would likely have more satisfying lives with other people, and thus welcomed me unreservedly, helping to ease some of the awkward tension in those early days when we were all just getting used to the sudden plunge into each other's lives. Because of all this, the transition to stepmother was an easy one, though I still cringe at that word. I'm hoping to make "slightly older female friend-like person" a thing.

That saying, "Be careful what you wish for because you just might get it"? Truth, but to that I'd add, "Be careful what you wish to avoid, because you're probably going to get that too." I got a companion. I also got a certain type of responsibility, the likes of which I'd been successfully avoiding for decades: the responsibility for lives that depended on me. No, I would not be responsible for raising children; Ken and his ex-wife had done all that already, and done it well. But it's no coincidence that I met his dog before I met him. With Ken, animals would come first.

One of the early tests of our relationship came when Ken went away for a conference and I took care of his pets. I should say right up front that three of the four pets he had at this time were animals he adopted in from the university's wildlife clinic, taking them on because they were not native to this area and could not be released back into the wild. These three were not the kinds of pets you play with. They were not even the kinds of pets you pet. Basically they were the kinds of pets your parents described when you clamored for a puppy as a child: never-ending drudgery centered entirely on bodily functions. There was a turtle, a tortoise (and I assumed at some point, dating a Vet-MD, I'd know the difference between those two), an anole (a type of lizard, the name of which I couldn't help work into certain profane limericks), and the dog, Cayenne. The dog, sweet-natured and generally well behaved, would be no problem at all. Yes, sometimes she got in the trash. Sometimes she slipped out the front door and went cavorting around the neighborhood, giving me and Ken anxiety attacks that she'd be hit by a car or eat something nasty. But these were rare occurrences; more commonly she would follow us around the kitchen while we cooked dinner and occasionally interpose herself between us and the stove while we boiled pasta or flipped pancakes. This was partially out of her usual need for affection but largely, of course, out of hunger for scraps that might fall, and I was always afraid of stumbling over her and sending dinner and dishes flying. (I mused about selling this idea to the Food Network as their latest silly cooking competition show: Animal in the Kitchen. Contestants have to prepare a three-course meal all while caring for a clingy, demanding critter. Here's the twist: turns out the judge of the contest is the critter itself. *Are YOU an Animal in the Kitchen?*)

The turtle and the tortoise lived in the basement, in large Nemo-themed kiddie pools under heat lamps. My duties to the shelled critters that week were easy: add water to their drinking basins and add food to their food bowls. The turtle was a carnivore and was served small dollops of canned dog food; the tortoise was vegan and received a nice organic salad mix. That was it. "They're boring," Ken conceded. "Pretty much living paperweights."

The anole was the high-maintenance one. "He hasn't eaten on his own for months," Ken informed me. "He has to be hand-fed." This entailed heating water, mixing it with powdered reptile feed, filling a syringe, and slowly, carefully, dropping the mixture down El Verde's mouth. His name made him sound like a tiny dictator, which I suppose he was in his own way, boss of his aquarium, never mind the absence of anyone to dictate to.

A few days before Ken left, we did a practice feeding so I could get comfortable with the process. He coached me through it: "Grasp him by the shoulders and take him out of the tank. His mouth should gape open automatically, which will make it easy to feed him. Be careful, though—he bites."

He didn't, though. Animals often seem to like me, even eating-disordered reptiles. I did everything just fine, Ken nodding his pleased approval, and carefully placed El Verde on a branch in his tank. El Verde went limp. He fell back from the branch, hung upside-down, rolled his eyes back in his head, and dropped to the floor of the tank.

Oh my god. I killed El Verde. "What's wrong with him?" I whispered hoarsely.

Ken peered into the tank. "He does look a little weird."

Oh crap. I didn't even pass the preliminaries. Oh crap oh crap oh crap.

Ken calmed me down. The lizard was very old, he explained, and could go any time. It was quite possible he might die in the week I was taking care of him. This did not comfort me. Even though I had no deep affection for the critter, I did not want El Verde to die. Ken spent a good ten minutes reassuring me I would not be responsible for anything that happened. I still dreaded having to deal with the little reptile's demise, but I also wanted to spare Ken from having to lug the tank over to the clinic so a vet student could deal with El Verde. In the end, I agreed to be his caretaker—though hopefully not his undertaker.

El Verde survived. In fact, once he finally resumed eating on his own, he got returned to his native Bayou when some of Ken's students drove down there to do field research. We joked that as soon as he was let go, some predator probably gulped him up. We joked, because that's what you do when something you've spent time with and thus come to care about is now out of your control. I hope he did OK out there, and I'm glad he lived long enough under my care to go home again.

The biggest test, of course, was yet to come.

CHAPTER 3

Boston and Phoenix

IN SEPTEMBER 2014, BARELY a month after I moved in with him, Ken and I drove six hours to Flint, Michigan. Anyone can do a weekend in a fun city or a lovely lakeshore, but we tend to do things a little differently. "Next week: Elizabeth, New Jersey," I joked on our way. "I hear the factory plumes are gorgeous this time of year."

Actually, we were en route to pick up two parrots. Ken is not just any old vet-MD: he treats all sorts of animals but he's a bird specialist, a well-regarded one, and he had always wanted parrots, specifically macaws. Hence, Flint. The American auto industry may be down and out, but there's always exotic birds.

Before we hit the road, we had to get in our long runs for the week. He was doing twenty miles, as his target marathon was a month sooner than mine; I only did fourteen. (Yes, "only." Distance running is awesome for people who like to beat themselves up both mentally and physically.) The dog came with us, even though those distances may have been prohibitive to other canines her age. That morning she did fifteen good strong miles. As Ken was starting his fourth and final five-mile loop, he looked back and noticed the dog wasn't with him. He ran back to the car and saw her sitting there calmly. He called to her. She gave him a look that said, quite clearly, "Nuh uh. You may continue, foolish human; I am done here." It isn't often that the canine has more sense than we do, but when she does, she makes us look like dufuses.

As we made our way to Flint, I wondered how much of a dufus I would look like when our two new feathered friends joined us. So far, I'd had partial care of Ken's small menagerie and had managed not to kill anyone, though it was close with the lizard. Sometimes I struggled to get my own sorry self to function adequately. To add responsibility for someone else—be they furry, scaly, shelled or feathered—well, there was potential to send me over the edge. What's more, these were very young birds, still in the process of being weaned. Yes, birds are weaned; the term isn't exclusive to mammals but refers to any young animal's transition from being parent-fed to independent feeding. Instead of milk, macaws get a special formula that mimics the partially digested, regurgitated food they'd normally get from a parent. The unweaned macaws would be extremely high maintenance for a while, then they would only be very high maintenance for the rest of their lives.

I joked to Ken, regarding the oblivious dog, that she had no idea what she was in for. I was secretly referring to myself. Cayenne would probably be affected very little. There'd be strange new creatures stealing attention that formerly belonged to her, yes, but what she lost in belly-rub time she'd gain in treats dropped by her new roommates. I had no clear notion of what I would gain or lose. I only knew for certain that things were about to change a great deal.

When we reached the house of the bird lady in Flint, we were greeted at the door by a yappy dog so small I nearly stepped on him by accident, and so loud that had I not been a dog lover, the nearly-stepping-on might have been intentional. Later I would recognize one of the early sounds our parrots made as an imitation of this yapping beast. Parrots are astonishing mimics. More than one of Ken's clients have come to him worried that their pet was sick only for him to discover that the "coughing" and "sneezing" were simply the bird imitating the human. The Flint bird lady had an African grey she'd gotten as a rescue bird from a guy who traveled a lot and left the bird at home alone with nothing but a dead-battery smoke detector for company. Not surprisingly, the grey's most common sound was that awful high-pitched chirp. It was uncanny, perfectly reproduced, and every bit as annoying as the real thing. (There was only one other thing that came out of the grey's beak while we were there, apparently the only other thing he learned from his former owner. Quite out of the blue, in a deep and ugly male voice, the grey said "FUCK." That word hardly has much shock value any more given its ubiquity, but I was *completely* creeped out.)

Ken had decided on two different macaws: a blue-and-gold and a green-wing. Blue-and-golds really are blue and gold, but green-wings are mostly bright red, with just a band of green on the wings (singled out in the name to differentiate them from the very similar scarlet macaws). Prior to our picking up our birds, the breeder had been sending Ken videos of them so we could see that they were healthy and being cared for. Most of the videos focused on the green-wing, attractive and strong right from the start. He was clearly the bird lady's favorite, and she cooed over him endlessly. He even had another bird buddy, a cute little white-bellied caique who seemed inseparable from his big red pal. "Aw, they're gonna miss each other," Ken said, wistfully adding, "I wish *our* two were like that together." The blue-and-gold, however, had been slower to develop, and appeared more subdued in the videos when he appeared at all. The bird lady looked to be in her mid-30s, with the air of a faded former prom queen, and she must have had children; there were a few scattered kid toys among the great many bird toys, and I wondered if she played favorites as much with them. For their sake I hoped not, but it sure did seem like the green wing was the one who got straight As and lettered in every sport while the blue-and-gold was the one who ... didn't.

Indeed, this developmental chasm was plain to see when we first met them. The green-wing took to Ken right away, strutting right up to him and onto his arm, much to Ken's delight. The blue-and-gold did no strutting, and even if he had, he still would have looked more pathetic than majestic. His feathers had not completely developed, and his crop—sort of like a waiting room for a bird's stomach—stuck out baldly and grotesquely from his chest, as though he'd swallowed a ping-pong ball. He also displayed some baby-bird "tics"—awkward-looking repetitive mannerisms like nodding the head or swaying back and forth—that the green-wing had already outgrown. In other words, he looked pretty sad. Right away he became my favorite.

I didn't handle either of them that day, though; I stood back and let Ken take charge. He was the bird expert. I myself had never been this close to birds this large in my life. They were only four months old, but their beaks looked the size of lobster claws, with that much potential bone-cracking strength. Still, they had that adorably vulnerable look of young animals, huge eyes taking in everything around them.

Ken named them Boston and Phoenix, Boston because the Boston Marathon's colors are blue and gold, and Phoenix because he wanted to go with another city name and Phoenix is just an all-around good name for a bird. Tokyo might have worked too since their first language lessons from us were inadvertently in Japanese.

On the drive back from Michigan, Ken had his iPod on shuffle, and every now and then one of his "Learn Japanese" tracks would come on (remnant from a time when he thought he might travel to Tokyo for a conference). One minute, Ozzy Osbourne was encouraging us to go off the rails on a crazy train, the next we were asking *"Ima nanji desu ka?"* so we wouldn't miss said train. Because of this, I liked to think their first words would end up being *"Irasshai mase!"* That's the greeting the sushi chefs shout at you whenever you enter a Japanese restaurant—basically "WELCOME!!!" It's certainly better than the f-bomb.

The macaws did not end up speaking any Japanese, either then or later. They were mostly quiet on the ride back home, understandably freaked out by the sudden strangeness going on around them. "It'll be OK," I soothed. "We're going home."

✿

MANY PEOPLE WHO DECIDE to get a pet make lists of qualities they want in their new best buddy. Breed, size, age, personality traits—all of those tend to be considerations. As a veterinarian with an avian specialty, Ken had a different set of criteria, with a focus on what we offered them rather than what they offered us. There were certain things we had to provide in order to live with macaws.

Item One: The Social Aspect. Macaws are social animals, meaning they thrive far better with companions than without. No person can be with a pet all the time, no matter how devoted or unemployed, so this meant getting at least two.

Item Two: Weaning into Foraging. Once our birds were weaned, we needed to transition them right to foraging. There were to be no dishes of free food lying around. The habitat we created had to challenge them, allow them to work their minds, beaks, and claws, in order to eat.

Item Three: Enough Space to Fly.

Item Four: Positive Reinforcement Training.

More on these last two later.

Before bringing them home, we'd made sure the macaws had a suitable habitat so that they could become foragers. This had been a huge undertaking. The biggest premade birdcage is a tiny fraction of the size of the habitat Ken wanted for the boys. The space needed to be big enough that they could do short flights, as well as have plenty of room for climbing around and foraging. That meant we had to build it.

Finding suitable building materials took some creativity. The walls had to be made of something durable—those beaks could rip apart a lot of wire cages like they were made of tissue paper—as well as affordable, since we'd need a *lot* of it. Further, they could not be made of any material containing zinc, which is toxic to birds. And zinc is an ingredient not just in throat lozenges but also in many commercial metal products.

Ken found a solution: epoxy-coated linen shelving. The wires were thick enough so that they couldn't easily be beak-broken, and they were spaced such that macaw heads couldn't get stuck, plus the epoxy coating meant no exposed zinc. We bought every shelf Menard's had in stock. All of them. I imagined running into people we knew at the checkout aisles and trying to explain. "We have a *lot* of linens. We're, like, collectors. With some folks it's stamps or coins; with us it's pillowcases and duvet covers."

The next problem was how to attach the shelves to each other—and keep them attached. Back to Menard's. First Ken tried zip ties. They were cheap and worked fairly well until they didn't. After a few months, chew-happy Phoenix figured out how to gnaw through them. Next up were these metal brackets called hog rings—I have no idea why, as they didn't seem to have anything to do with hogs—but they were sturdier than the zip ties and still sans zinc. And then a few months after *that* Ken announced the linen shelving had to go. The boys' tails were getting ratty from climbing the walls, plus Phoenix was starting to figure out how to pop the hog rings. At one point a section of the cage's roof fell in because Phoenix had taken apart all the ties, and he and Boston had gotten out to explore the rest of the basement. Next up: big sheets of corrugated metal, fashioned into an even larger cage, now more appropriately termed a *room*. All of this construction and reconstruction involved lifting heavy things and making lots of noise with tools, as well as cursing a lot. Before long, the boys added certain colorful new words to their vocabularies.

The bird room took up nearly half the basement, a good 400-plus square feet, larger than my studio apartment in Manhattan. In it there were dozens of toys, foragers, and perches, almost all of which Ken had constructed himself. Store-bought stuff just didn't cut it; even toys designed for larger birds with strong beaks tended to last no more than a few hours tops. Instead, Ken scoured websites for appropriate toy materials he could buy cheap in bulk quantities—bamboo poles, coconut shells, sisal rope, vine balls, braided raffia—while instructing me not to get rid of any old boxes, plastic soda bottles, or cardboard tubes from paper towels and toilet paper. They could all be made into foragers. As for perches, after seeing a lot of downed trees on a trail run, Ken kept a handsaw in the car so he could gather suitable branches whenever we came across them. "Perches," he'd say every time we saw a fallen sycamore or a leaf-bare elm. "So many perches."

Ken built another innovative, and quite different, construction for our boys. He had requested that the breeder abstain from clipping their flight feathers. The practice of feather-clipping is common because many owners of macaws can't realistically deal with a large flighted bird in their homes.

Birds crash into windows and knock things over. If the bird never learns to fly, it can be taken out of its cage from time to time or even kept in an open stand. It doesn't hurt the bird physically—only the feathers are clipped, so it's about as painful as clipping a toenail—but if it's done before the bird fledges, the bird will likely never learn to fly. Ken wanted our macaws to fly. He was therefore understandably irked when he discovered that first day that the breeder had gone ahead and clipped a few of their flight feathers anyway. Apparently Phoenix had given her a scare when he almost flew right into a glass window. She decided it wasn't worth the risk to grant Ken's request. The feathers would grow out eventually when the boys molted, but this might set them back from being able to fly—to the point where they might never gain the necessary skills.

Solution: while they waited for their own feathers to come in, they could borrow some. The procedure is called imping, and it involves temporarily grafting another, similar bird's feathers onto the hollow shaft where the clipped feathers had been. Ken had all sorts of feathers left by avian patients at the clinic, so all he had to do was attach feather to shaft using a small connector, in this case a section of bamboo skewer with epoxy on the ends. When the boys molted, the grafted feathers would fall out naturally. It was weird but it worked, and it allowed Boston and Phoenix to fledge right on schedule.

I very much enjoyed the novelty of those early days. It was fun to go down to the basement in the morning with my coffee and watch them explore their habitat. It was exciting when Ken brought them upstairs so they could stretch their wings. The house had a foyer open to the second floor, with an odd atrium above the front door that I guess was meant for decorations, though Ken had kept it empty until we got the boys. Their ability to fly up and down would be crucial going forward, he asserted, and it wasn't one that tended to develop quickly or easily. To help them in this regard, he installed a wood pole for a perch in the atrium, as well as a few wood blocks and coconut shells, and began training the boys to fly up to it and back down to his hand.

It became a regular routine. I'd pour myself a glass of red wine and we'd sit together in the stairwell for an hour or so before dinnertime. "Boston," he called, and after a bit of hesitation, the blue-and-gold bird fluttered down to him. Ken gave him a small treat (their favorites were these fruit-shaped pellets that looked like Lucky Charms cereal), and lifted his arm so that Boston would fly back to the perch. "Phoenix." And after a lot of hesitation—oddly, bigger, healthier Phoenix was the more cautious of the two when it came to trying new things—the big red bird would do the same. Sometimes Ken would give the flight practice a rest and we would just sit there, close to each other, watching them chomping at their toys or tussling playfully with each other or even sliding down the banister on their claws.

I thought, *This is nice. I could get used to this.*

CHAPTER 4

Bite Club

THE FEAR OF BEING bitten is instinctive and primal. I don't think you have to be bitten first to have this fear, unlike with some other painful and scary things, like being burned. Moreover, you don't get over it quickly. When I started trail running and fell down a lot, people told me I'd get used to it. I didn't. I'm more afraid of falling now than ever—you should see me in winter on ice, waddling like a penguin. Same thing goes for bites. The first time Phoenix latched onto my finger with his beak was a shock, and the subsequent times did not seem like playful nips that I laughed off or ignored entirely. I remained wary around him, wondering if a falconer's glove might be a worthwhile investment—or possibly a suit of mail.

I did not have any such garments, alas, and to be fair, the "bites" I got from Phoenix (for it was pretty much always him) weren't necessarily intended as such. Sometimes he simply needed to hold onto something to get him where he wanted to be, and since wings are useless for all but flying and claws don't have a very far reach, a macaw's beak does what hands do for us. Obviously, if you work with animals for a living, you've gotten used to all this—though even Ken will not try to convince you that the sensation of beak closing on finger is easy to shrug off. It hurts. It's scary, too, to realize that those same beaks closing lightly over your finger can snap tree branches and coconut shells and rip chunks out of thick PVC pipes. Still, I knew it was illogical to be so much more afraid of the macaws than of the random dogs I encountered on running trails. A macaw can break your finger or tear your earlobe, but a dog can take your whole hand, or your face—or your life, quite possibly. Yes, *Cujo* was fiction (not one of King's better efforts, either) and dog maulings are rare, but they do happen. Yet dogs were more of a known thing to me, their behavior easier to read and deal with. When I'm reaching my hand toward a bird with a treat, it's often difficult to know whether that bird will take it gently or lunge and snap at me. I'd noticed that Cayenne often watched my hands very intently; to her, hands were what gave treats and belly rubs—instruments of pleasure. With Boston and Phoenix, my hands had become something else: targets.

In short, I was afraid of them for a while, especially Phoenix, to the point where I did not want anything to do with them—something I had to admit to myself even if I didn't want to admit it just yet to Ken.

It wasn't only bite-phobia that kept me at a distance from the macaws. I did not know what to do with them even when they were behaving well. I could take walks with the dog, run with her, play rope-toy-tug with her, pet her, teach her easy tricks, or just sit reading while she lay comfortably at my feet. The birds, I could give treats. That was about it, and that got boring very quickly—for all three of us.

It's understandable why tortoises live so long. When you move that slowly, you'd better have a lot of time ahead of you so that you don't spend your whole life within a three-foot radius of the place you were born (though they pretty much do that anyway). This logic doesn't work at all for macaws, who are also long-lived—almost as long as humans—but not at all slow. Macaws don't just fly; they're flighty. Ours seemed unable to focus on one thing for very long without getting distracted. Phoenix's diligent munching on vegetables was about the only time he finished a task he started. The rest of the time he and Boston went from sparring with each other to preening each other to seizing a chunk of wood and making toothpicks out of it, all within a couple minutes' time. Every interaction I had with them in those early days began with anxiety—would I lose a finger?—then, if all went well, progressed to a slightly tense pleasure when they took the treats nicely from me before cascading back into anxiety. *Now what?*

When I mentioned to people that we had macaws, I was initially surprised how many of them said, "Wow! That's great! I'm afraid of birds!" And they weren't just talking about big, potentially pain-inflicting parrots but apparently the entire avian collective. (My mother was one of the exceptions. Her first reaction: "You let them fly around the house? Don't they poop on everything?" After I assured her that they were very clean animals who liked to poop only in certain places, she seemed fine with them.) Even after my own initially harrowing experiences, I didn't completely understand other people's fear. After all, a picture of a macaw is unlikely to make someone instinctively flinch the way a spider or a snake or a Grizzly bear might. But I guess Alfred Hitchcock was onto something. People generally seem neutral to positive about birds from afar, but up close, there's something unfathomable about them that provokes wariness. They can be hard to read, with facial features that remain rigid compared to many mammals', beaks that never crack a smile or a frown, eyes that don't shift in their sockets and thus always seem fixed on whatever is ahead. Perhaps it's also that they are so much closer to reptiles than mammals, making them more alien to us. They certainly seemed alien to me.

Frankly I would have been content to view the macaws from afar. It was fun watching them climb around their cage like feathered monkeys, tussling like brothers—big brother Phoenix often playfully tormenting kid brother Boston, who nevertheless followed the red bird around like a shadow—but Ken wanted them to be more than the feathered equivalent of tropical fish. They were meant to be interactive pets, he believed, just like dogs or horses. He was comfortable interacting with them himself. You never think of a bird as cuddly, the way a puppy or a bunny or some other furry mammalian pet might be, but Phoenix frequently became a big goo-goo-eyed baby in his arms. Boston, always the more aloof of the two, would look on with faint disdain, but even he allowed Ken to stroke him on occasion. I knew it could be done, but given my early experiences with them, I wasn't sure how willing I was to endure the beakiness to cuddle them myself.

Having only ever dealt with pets with a fairly limited lifespan compared to mine, it took a while for me to fully grasp that Boston and Phoenix would be ours *for the rest of our lives.* I knew macaws lived a long time, but I was stunned when the implications of that knowledge sank in. You don't like to think that a dog may be with you for only a dozen years or so, maybe up to twenty if it's a smaller breed. Ken's kids howled in horrified denial when he reminded them that Cayenne would likely only live another year or two, tops. He was just being realistic, of course, but they had grown up with her, so it was hard for them to admit that she wouldn't always be around somewhere sniffing at something disgusting and trying to eat it. With that in mind, you'd think it would be a relief to know that at least *these* pets would likely outlive us. It wasn't exactly a relief. I wouldn't say it was a burden—avoiding dealing with death any more than necessary suited me fine—but I wondered how I'd feel about the macaws in ten years, in twenty, when they were still young and healthy and we weren't anything close to that.

But Boston and Phoenix would probably be with us until death (our own) did us part, so I had to figure out how to deal with them.

Ken encouraged me to try getting one of them to step up onto my arm, something he'd mastered on Day One. Thing is, sometimes the birds "stepped" not with their feet but with their beaks. Even though this was mostly for balance, and their grip on my radius and ulna wasn't hard, it was difficult to avoid cringing as soon as a feathered head stretched forward. I tried wearing thick long-sleeved shirts, even in hot weather, as protection. "That actually makes it worse," Ken insisted. "They'll grab at the cloth and not realize they're also grabbing skin."

I looked at him the way you look at someone who tells you it would be better if you do the one thing you absolutely don't want to do because any other way makes it worse—like that person who insists you drink something hot if you want to cool off in warm weather. (The idea is hot liquid makes you sweat, and the evaporation of sweat from skin cools the body. So ... if you're hot, you should make your body *even hotter*—which assumes you aren't *already* sweating from the heat that drove you to seek a refreshing beverage in the first place. Just bring me a cold one.) I was sure he had a point, but I didn't care. The idea of my vulnerable skin exposed to their beaks and claws made me nervous as hell.

Being comfortable in my own body has taken me a long time to accomplish, and I'm still not completely there. When I go trail running, there are moments I feel strong and confident and sure. Such moments are almost inevitably followed by my feet catching a root or a rock or each other and my wobbling and stumbling and flailing. Gravity has a way of reminding you how little control you have, and while macaws are a less pervasive force in the universe, they have a similar effect. It seemed I was always standing the wrong way, moving the wrong way, standing again the wrong way, and my arms, head, fingers, neck, and eyes were never where they were supposed to be. I was beginning to feel like some anatomical freak—which, to them, I suppose I was.

"Bend your elbow. Don't hold your arm straight or they'll climb up to your shoulder and you have less control that way."

I received these instructions like a self-conscious klutz trying to learn the latest dance moves, awkwardly positioning my body the way he suggested. When Boston or Phoenix finally climbed on my arm and stayed there, I experienced approximately three seconds of elation before our eyes met and I panicked. "OK. I did it. Um, take him back. Please. Like, *now*."

I knew Ken was disappointed that I wasn't trying harder to work with the birds. Though I didn't want to disappoint him, I'd reached a point in my life where I needed other people's approval less than I once had. I mostly wanted to put a good faith effort into something that clearly meant a lot to him. I wanted to try, but I also didn't want to fail and felt no need to try things I was pretty sure weren't going to work out. After nearly five decades of life, I knew myself reasonably well: knew my strengths and weaknesses, knew what I was and wasn't capable of. While I'd never encountered a situation like this one, I suspected it would take more patience, coordination, bravery, and thick skin (literally and figuratively) than I possessed—and, at my age, would likely ever possess.

It was a bit of a relief when I realized that it wasn't just me getting nipped. Ken had to deal with it as well. As soon as he came home from work, he would change from his work clothes into "an ugly sweatshirt," as he put it—something old without buttons or zippers that Phoenix would eagerly destroy—and get the boys out, inevitably followed by a litany of "no" and "drop it" and "let go." Fingers, nose, earlobes, hair—if it could be reached by a beak, it would be. Of course, rather than flinching, freezing, or whimpering *get him off me get him off me*, Ken tried to make these into teachable moments following the Point Four concept of positive reinforcement. This is slightly more complicated than the name would suggest. "Reinforcement" is what you do when you want the bird to keep doing a certain behavior, as opposed to "punishment," which is what you do when you want the bird to stop doing something. Meanwhile, "positive" in this case doesn't necessarily mean good so much as giving something, while "negative" means taking away something. Doing the math yields four combinations, each one useful in different situations. Positive reinforcement means giving the animal something (like a treat) to encourage a certain behavior (like saying hello, for a macaw, or lifting a paw to "shake," for a dog). This also happens to be the method that many bird experts believe has the least potential for the animal to feel threatened. As such, this was the method Ken wanted to emphasize in his training.

This is easy enough to do when you are teaching the bird to do things like lift his claw so you can trim his nails. Ken had a lot of success with them in this regard. "High four!" he'd say, and one of the macaws would lift a claw to clap against his hand. "Other foot!" and the bird would switch to the other claw. "Spin!" and around he'd go, in a slow-motion avian pirouette. These may have seemed like silly pet tricks, but having an animal perform certain specific activities enables a veterinarian to do a more thorough checkup without being too pushy. Sometimes we'd catch Boston quietly saying these things to himself and going through the motions— "Other foot," left claw up, "other foot," right claw up, "spin" and around he would go—like a perfectionist actor going over a part.

Positive reinforcement becomes a little tougher when the bird does something you don't want it to do, like bite. If you want to reinforce, rather than punish, the idea is to get the bird to do something he can be rewarded for, as a substitute for the undesirable behavior. Now, anyone who has *tried* to use positive reinforcement in any situation, from stubborn child to nippy pet, knows how impossible this theory becomes when you attempt to put it into practice.

A large red bird has the two halves of his beak on either side of your index finger, and you've just seen that same beak crush a hazelnut into powder, and you've just said *LET GO* as patiently as you can and all he's done is eye you mischievously as if to see how many more times he can make you say it—well, who on earth is going to have the presence of mind to think of some kind of "positive behavior" you can encourage the beast to do instead? Not me, certainly, and many times not Ken either, despite his best efforts. This did not make me feel better at all. If even Ken couldn't keep Phoenix from beaky behavior, what hope did I have?

But as always, and true to his hard-core distance running nature, Ken persisted, a lot more than I did, because he had a bigger goal than just getting along with the macaws. With big goals come big risks—in this case, risks that were bigger than bites.

CHAPTER 5

Flight Club

THE FIRST THING MOST people ask when they see you have parrots is, "Do they talk?" Ken always answered this question honestly and patiently, though to him this was like asking a dog owner if Fido could walk on his hind legs. It's possible, sure, but you don't get a dog so that they'll walk like a human. Likewise, to him macaws were not about talking—the breeds he'd chosen tend not to be great talkers anyway—but about flying. People can talk, and in his mind I suspect this was not one of their more endearing qualities. People can't fly, and flying was what he wanted to experience, if vicariously through these birds.

It's probably good that Ken didn't care about their talking, since their first words had been the extremely boring "hi" and "hello" and they didn't go all that much further in building a repertoire. (Boston from time to time would say something that sounded like "algorithm," though I have no idea what it really might have been. "Algorithm" is not something Ken or I say, like, ever. Perhaps the bird breeder was into S&M and that was her safe word.) What the macaws lacked in vocabulary, they made up for in volume. We were lucky our dog was deaf. Many times when Boston and Phoenix screeched at us, the dog would look at us ponderously, appearing to wonder why we were gritting our teeth and covering our ears.

Ken did not waste time trying to teach them clever things to say. As soon as they reached the age to fledge, he wanted to teach them to fly. Difficult, given that he can't fly, and a little curious that he should be so enamored of bird flight. He did not feel that way about flight in general. Like many people, he hated having to travel by commercial jet, squashed in those cramped seats with no legroom, elbow of a stranger in your ribs. He also—thank goodness—had no interest in things like skydiving or hang-gliding. If one of those had been his obsession, it might have been a deal-breaker for me, but luckily we established fairly early in our relationship that he felt the same way I did about jumping out of planes or off cliffs: an emphatic *oh hell no.* Although he did not necessarily want to fly himself, he wanted, perhaps, to get as close to a pure flight experience as possible. People can't fly; birds can. Because an imitation of flight did not interest him, and because he couldn't be a bird, he sought the closest approximation he could get.

He had a grand plan, too: to take the macaws to the places we went running and let them fly while we ran. This was ambitious, to say the least. The places where we run are full of tall trees, rolling hills and valleys, all of which can make things difficult for a runner and really difficult for a runner who is trying to keep sight of two parrots. It was stressful enough when the dog got out and went gallivanting around the neighborhood; with birds there's a whole other dimension into which they can disappear. There were also hawks and hunters and who knew what else. But "free flight" is a thing among parrot enthusiasts, it seems, and Ken was determined to make it *our* thing.

He signed up for a reputable online class in free-flying birds, which to me seemed like signing up for a reputable online class in water skiing. Can that *really* be sufficient preparation? Regardless, the class was well organized and clear, with all sorts of useful information that made the enterprise seem as straightforward as I knew it could not possibly be. For example, there were five different classifications for areas to fly: Level 1 is an area where sight lines are good for quite some distance and there is little to nothing that a bird could get stuck in (like tall trees) or could land on and not be retrievable (like a lake), while Level 5 is basically the Grand Canyon, or its equivalent. By that point you totally trust your birds to fly free, knowing they have the skills to deal with obstacles and challenges—and knowing they will be able to come back to you.

But before we even got to Level 1, we needed to get them outside. This alone was more than most pet parrots, eternally encaged, would ever experience. It was also probably more stress than any pet parrot owner should ever put themselves through. After quite a bit of research, Ken got some falcon jesses—leashes that attached to a bird's legs with long cords—making sure to find ones that were lightweight and springy but also durable, because, well, everything they could get their beaks on had to be durable. Predictably, they hated the jesses, tried to chew them off immediately. The jesses weren't likely painful or even uncomfortable, but they were a strange new thing, and Phoenix in particular had one standard reaction to new things: destroy them.

The jesses were impractical for other reasons. They tangled easily and were so short that the boys could do barely more than a hop to a perch in the yard. They could fly farther than that in their cage, so what was the point? At least in their cage, I reminded Ken testily, they couldn't *keep* flying, the way they could if they were outside and untethered. He made a firm decision: the jesses would come off.

The moment we removed the jesses was terrifying. If one of the boys took off, he could be out of sight in less than a minute. After just a few minutes, he could be a mile away. It was unlikely either of them had the ability to fly continuously for a mile at the moment, but that hardly mattered. We lived in a subdivision named Savannah Green. If the area had been true to its name, we'd have less to worry about since sight lines in a savannah would be good, but like most subdivisions, ours seemed to have been named randomly. All around our house there were many other houses in close proximity. Two birds could get lost in suburbia very, very quickly.

To minimize the risk, Ken dealt with each bird separately. If Phoenix went off-leash, Boston stayed on. Boston, despite having been runty and slower to develop as a hatchling, had proven to be a better climber and faster to master short indoor flights. He went off-leash first. In retrospect, I wonder what would have happened if Ken had picked Phoenix, physically stronger since the beginning, to go first. But he hadn't. He picked Boston.

At first everything went all right. Boston took short training flights from a makeshift outdoor perch (branches stuck in a Christmas tree stand steadied with rocks) to Ken's arm and back. Then something spooked Boston and he took off. We never figured out what it was—we never knew what might freak them out on any given day, whether it was because Ken had a new hat on or because some terrifying little butterfly landed on a flower a few feet away. Big things like noisy trucks might go by without so much as a twitch, but heaven forbid I should remove my glasses to clean some shmutz off them. Sheer pandemonium.

So it had happened, what I'd feared the most: Boston was gone. Of course, given his limited flight ability, he couldn't have gone far, and given the volume of his screeching, he would at least be traceable. Ken leapt over our fence and took off after him, yelling at me to stay there in case Boston circled back. That would have been great, but it didn't happen. Eventually Ken found him in a tall tree out in front of the house. The good news was he'd been found close by. There was also, of course, bad news.

There's an interesting article by Malcolm Gladwell about the difference between choking and panicking. When someone chokes—usually an athlete—they become too conscious and deliberate of their actions rather than relying on muscle memory. Panic is the opposite. A creature that panics reverts to instinct instead of thinking out the logical next move. Deer freeze in car headlights because their instinct when faced with potential danger is to stay very still, even though this is the worst thing they could do in this particular situation. Ditto, apparently, a fledgling macaw. The thing Boston needed to do when he sensed potential danger was to come back to Ken. His instincts, however, told him that getting up in a tall tree and staying there was the answer. And that's what he did.

Ken called. He made the "come here" gesture, sort of like a one-handed "jazz hands" but with fingers together. He held up treats. He went away and came back. He brought Phoenix over and fed Phoenix treats. Look what big brother gets! You could get that too! Boston stayed put.

It was early evening in summer, and there were a lot of kids out playing on the sidewalks, which meant that pretty soon there were a lot of kids gathered around us pointing and gasping and waving to the blue-and-gold bird in the tree. We didn't want to be mean to the kids—this was probably the most exciting thing to happen in this neighborhood all year—but they were making things worse. There was no way an already freaked-out Boston would fly down to Ken when he was surrounded by small, exuberant strangers.

Eventually the kids got called in to dinner, which made things a little easier—but also more urgent. The sun would be setting soon. Once it started getting darker, Boston would not move an inch until sunrise the next morning. The night was supposed to be a mild one weather-wise, so he wouldn't freeze, but he'd be thirsty and hungry and potentially vulnerable to anything that *did* fly at night, like an owl. Granted, there weren't likely to be many owls lurking in Savannah Green, but he was still defenseless and exposed, and there would be nothing we could do about it.

Ken got out a stepladder, stood on the highest rung and called again. The distance between Boston and Ken's arm couldn't have been much greater than the distance the boys would fly inside the house from the atrium, but that was a known situation and this was not. There were branches in the way, and strange noises and movements, and Boston had no idea what might happen next. Neither did we.

What did happen when Boston finally took flight was exactly what we did *not* want to happen: instead of coming down to Ken's arm, he flew up and away, squawking fearfully, and in no time at all he'd gone out of sight again.

Ken took off running, yelling at me to get my car and drive further out in case Boston had *really* taken off. He'd seen the general direction the bird had gone, but in that general direction there were any number of places he could be. Up and down the blocks I drove, creeping along with all the windows open, listening and looking, hoping nobody called the cops thinking I was some kind of stalker. I hoped even more that I'd come across Ken with Boston back on his arm and this nightmare would be over.

It wasn't over. Not even close.

We didn't find Boston before nightfall. He had stopped vocalizing long ago, so we couldn't follow his cries, and even if we tracked him down, we wouldn't be able to retrieve him. Ken had a general idea where he might be—clear out of our own subdivision, which was a newer one, into the next, which was older with much more mature trees. Boston liked being high up—if Phoenix was on one perch in the bird room, Boston always wanted to find a higher one—and that meant that even on the fully extended ladder, Ken would likely be unable to get anywhere near him. But none of that mattered until we found him. Boston was out there alone and likely terrified, and we still didn't know where.

We went home in silence. I checked when sunrise would be and we set our phone alarms for a half hour before that time. Neither of us got any sleep.

The next morning, we rose before our alarms and gathered anything we might need: flashlights, bird treats, water bottles, ropes, binoculars. The dog seemed excited—*are we going on an adventure?*—then dismayed when we did not appear to be bringing her along. "Sorry, Cayenne," I said as we were leaving, and added mentally, *At least* you *always come back.* Cayenne looked up at me, uncomprehending, still hopeful. *So, we're going on an adventure now, right?*

We returned to the area where Ken suspected Boston might be—and there he was. Good news! Yes, there he was, way up high, surrounded by branches and leaves, impossible for us to reach. Bad news. As the sun rose, flocks of little birds began to appear. They were not happy with this strange-looking intruder in their tree, and made it very clear they wanted him gone.

Worse news. Boston took off again, heading even further away from home.

We tracked him again—Ken running, me driving, again listening, searching, again feeling helpless dread. This was not going to end well, I was sure of it. How could it be otherwise? How the hell were we going to get him back?

When we found him again, he'd gotten himself into yet another tall tree, though this one afforded us a better view of him from across the street and

there was a clear path for him to fly down to us. All
he had to do was take that path.

Boston didn't move.

Ken had to get to work at the university. I worked
from home and didn't have any deadlines that day.
Boston was almost certainly not going to fly down
to me—he had only trained for flying with Ken—
but there was one way I could help. "I'll watch him,"
I told Ken.

A flicker of relief crossed his face. "Call me if he
leaves the tree. Well, follow him first, then call me."
With one last anxious look at his bird buddy, Ken
left for work.

You've probably heard the simile "like watching
paint dry" to describe something boring. This was
infinitely duller—yet insanely stressful at the same
time. I couldn't do anything but stare at the tree,
for what ended up being hours, because I was afraid
that if I looked away for even a few seconds, Boston
would take off and I'd miss seeing where he went.
So I sat in my car and stared at the blue-and-gold
spot amidst the leaves and wondered over and over
how the hell it had come to this.

When Ken finally got a break from work he took
over tree-watching duties and sent me home to take

care of the dog and myself. An hour or so later, he returned as well. "I got him," he announced as soon as he came through the door. "He finally flew down to me."

It seemed almost anticlimactic after all that drama, but that was fine with me. My elation was short lived. I had barely managed to express my joy and ask about Boston's health before Ken added, "I guess I need to find a Level 1 spot."

In the back of my mind I had somehow imagined this would be the end of free flying. Of course it wasn't.

Even though we lived in the middle of rural Illinois, it was surprisingly difficult to find an appropriate Level 1 site. Most farmland, after all, is privately owned; you can't just wander into someone's soybean field and let loose the parrots. Ken settled on a bit of land in town owned by the university where he works. We figured if anyone asked, he *is* a university employee, he *does* work at the vet clinic, and therefore his flying of macaws on university property constitutes valuable research on behalf of this magnificent institute of higher education. Sure. Anyway, it worked pretty well for a Level 1 site, at least for Phoenix, who made some successful first flights. As for Boston, he seemed reluctant to fly at all other than short hops from Ken to a standing perch. This was understandable, and perfectly fine with me. It was less fine with Ken, but he figured there was no point in pushing it. Boston would fly again when he was ready.

So that Boston could be with Ken while Phoenix flew, Ken fashioned a "backpack perch" made from an old hydration pack he used to run with during ultras. He took out the water container and substituted a T-shaped PVC pipe wrapped with sisal rope. Boston could stand on the pipe, jesses on and clipped to the pack, while Ken walked around. Ken also had a "treat pouch"—a waist pack that was actually a rock climber's chalk pack, in this case filled with nuts and pellets as well as a target stick and clicker. All this plus his safari hat and he was fully outfitted—"the biggest bird nerd in the world," as he put it.

Phoenix made impressive progress, but more importantly, he seemed to be enjoying himself. His flights not only became longer and stronger, they were more playful. He went zooming away with the wind behind him, made a sharp turn, and then descended slowly against the wind back to Ken, floating down like a hummingbird. When he took off again, he went "jinking," tilting and veering rapidly left and right like a fighter pilot. Sometimes he flew low to the ground and looked at stuff below him. When he flew by me, he gave me a glance as if to say, "Oh, hello, fancy meeting you here!" before zooming away. He soared in the sunlight, feathers iridescent. He was having fun, and so was Ken. "I will *never* get tired of this," Ken beamed as Phoenix landed perfectly on his arm again.

There were a few minor mishaps. At one point, flying too long and running out of energy, Phoenix landed in the middle of the cornfield and Ken had to wade in after him. It's no wonder there are a fair number of horror movies with scenes in cornfields; they are ominous, and they can swallow a man whole. I stared at the spot where Ken had disappeared. This town is surrounded by cornfields. Inevitably, part of each day is spent looking at them, so my fixed, anxious gaze was bound to look strange. I waited, desperately trying to think of what I might say to any ag types who came around wondering why I was staring into the field (*oh, nothing, I just really love corn?*). Suddenly a man's fist popped up from the tassels, holding aloft a bright red bird. Soon thereafter the rest of the man emerged, his goofy safari hat askew. Beneath its brim he was grinning.

"Seen any baseball players in there?" I asked.

He shook his head: Nope, just one parrot, slightly lost but fine, and one parrot's person, hugely relieved.

I was relieved as well, but the relief, I knew, would be short-lived. The parrot's person would let go of the bird, the bird would fly away, and we would both be left standing there, waiting.

During another flight, Phoenix got chased relentlessly by a very persistent crow who clearly resented our intrusion in what he must have considered *his* cornfield. Crows are smaller than macaws, but if you've ever seen one picking at roadkill as you drove toward it, wondering when it was going to inevitably lose the game of chicken, wondering *if* it was even going to lose, then finally, just before you were sure you'd have to swerve, the crow sauntered nonchalantly away—well, you know how ballsy they are. When Phoenix finally made it safely back to Ken, he was clearly shaken. He was used to being Top Bird, Lord Master over cowering Boston. He had not expected his supremacy to be challenged so brazenly, and he did not like it. The crow circled back and landed on a post nearby, a shiny black wraith. Phoenix shrank back in the cage.

Research on crows suggests they have incredible memories, particularly for human faces as well as for other birds. If there was any reason to doubt that research, we could easily supply additional supporting evidence. The next time we went back to the field, a week or so later, as soon as we took the boys out, the wraith reappeared. My own memory for birds is extremely suspect so there was no guarantee that this was the same crow—but it almost certainly was. This was his field. He'd chased that big red interloper off before, and now he was ready to do it again. Perhaps macaws also have good memories, or at least have a normal response to a traumatic event, because as soon as Phoenix caught sight of the crow, he cowered again, refusing to leave Ken's arm. At that point we decided to graduate them to Level 2, earned or otherwise.

For Level 2, we took our bird buddies out to one of the far corners of our town, where some developers had been in the beginning stages of starting a new subdivision with yet another of those randomly generated names (some combination of glen / lake / hill / creek / green / vista / view / park) but never got beyond a road and a walking path before running out of money. A few tall trees grew here, and the interstate was disturbingly close, but not much else was potentially hazardous. What little there was, though, was enough. We spent hours searching the trees for one bird or the other that had gotten spooked mid-flight, anxious moments of hearing them calling but not knowing where they were, then not hearing them anymore, then finally spotting them and coaxing them down. It's surprisingly hard to get a macaw to fly downward, as down is where the nasty predators prowl, critters looking to leap upon a tasty avian meal. Up—up is where you want to be. Down, not so much—unless, wait! There's almond milk down there! (They *really* like almond milk, nut milks in general. The one time hazelnut milk was on sale and we got some for the boys, Phoenix looked like he was going to swoon. I swear he had the same rapturous response that certain people do when they eat Nutella.)

The time Boston flew off at Level 2, I was certain this would be the end. We were going to lose him forever. For hours we had no idea even where he was, as he'd stopped squawking completely. When I saw a car pull over to the shoulder of the interstate,

I knew it had to be because the driver was wondering what that particularly colorful bit of roadkill might be. When we had to go back home once it got dark, I steeled myself and tried all night to think of how to console Ken.

But it wasn't the end. The next morning we located him—clear on the other side of the interstate, in a tree in an office park, blessedly vacant for the weekend—and got him back. When Boston was good and ready (or hungry and thirsty) he would come down. And so far he had always come down, but in his own good time. This was not ideal. Macaws have not been domesticated, so while it's reasonable to expect a trained dog to come when called, since that's what they've been bred to do, a macaw pretty much has to want to come to you. There are ways to make this happen, and Phoenix fairly reliably came when Ken called (and often when Ken didn't call). Boston did not, and there often seemed little we could do about this.

Ken was not deterred. Boston would get there, he believed, and meanwhile Phoenix was a rock star. When Phoenix sprang into flight, it was exciting. It was also terrifying. "Your heart sinks and soars at the same time," as Ken put it. A bird in flight is doing what it was meant to do, what it loves to do, and it is beautiful and powerful doing it. But—that flight is also completely out of your control, as are other elements that might affect it. You can only watch, wait, and hope.

And, in my case, worry—a lot.

I worried about everything. I worried they'd get hit by a car. I worried about dogs and cats lunging from below, hawks pouncing from above, model airplane and drone enthusiasts deliberately crashing into them just for mean-spirited fun. I worried that the teenage boys next door who asked Ken how much birds like that cost would try to steal them so they could score some more pot, which they liked to smoke in their garage. In general I worried that we would lose them. I wasn't afraid that they'd deliberately leave us. Despite what people sometimes thought, they really did not have any desire to be "free" any more than the dog did. They'd been brought into the world by people and spent all their short lives being cared for by people, so I doubted that they'd believe there was any other choice. The problem wasn't that they were trying to get away from us; the problem, as I recognized with Boston that first time and every time after, was that they wanted to be with us, but they were birds. And the thing that birds do—fly—makes it difficult sometimes to be with people, especially when their flight skills are still developing. Think about the parent whose child gets out of sight for just a moment—the panic of it. In the time it takes a child to get out of sight, a bird could be a good half mile away from you, in a tree, on a rooftop, in a stranger's yard. That—that was what worried me. All of this stuff worried Ken as well, but lacking my deeply pessimistic nature, he shrugged his worries off and kept going.

Admirable. And stressful as hell.

I know it's impossible to avoid pain, but at that point in my life it still seemed feasible and desirable to sidestep *unnecessary* pain. And wouldn't you know it, into my world came a pair of sharp beaks and two pairs of sharp claws. They made it difficult to avoid pain and impossible to avoid drama. Would they fly, or would they be big stubborn duds who refused to leave the perch? Would they be quiet and gentle or squawky and nippy? Would they get lost, attacked, stuck in a tree? Would they enjoy their flight, or would this be the last time they ever flew again? It all seemed like such needless drama, and that was one thing I had decided I did not want.

CHAPTER 6

Needless Drama

LOVE IS DEPICTED ENDLESSLY as a fire, a fever, a madness. I went through all that when I was younger and discovered it wasn't really love, or at least not the kind of love that was good for me. I fell in love with Ken because he made me feel calm—a deeply satisfying calm of mind and body. If this sounds like the opposite of your idea of love, well, that's you; for me, there was a just-rightness about our feelings for each other that was exactly what I needed.

Believe it or not, his calm, rational demeanor frequently made me laugh. He claimed I was the only person who ever thought he was funny, that most everyone else considered him a very serious guy. Well, he was—but the serious was still hilarious.

Regarding the phrase "more fun than a barrel of monkeys," he commented: "A barrel is not a suitable habitat for a monkey, much less many monkeys."

Regarding the line in the Grinch song, "I'd pick the seasick crocodile": "A seasick crocodile would likely be completely incapacitated, thereby harmless."

Regarding the stereotypical pirate insult "you scurvy dog!": "Dogs manufacture their own vitamin C; therefore, they cannot get scurvy. More appropriate would be 'scurvy guinea pig.'" (It was even funnier when he said this in the slightly goofy voice he used when pretending it was Cayenne speaking.)

Ken is a man of science. I have a lot of respect for this, especially given that his profession is one fraught with passionate, righteously indignant, and frequently misinformed animal lovers. The first time we flew Phoenix at Level 2 some guy made it a point to march over to us and say "I think the trade in exotic birds is disgusting!" (Minutes later I came up with the stinging retort, "Oh yeah, well I think your face is disgusting!" but it was too late.)

The guy had a point: there was a time when many of the pet macaws in this country had been obtained illegally, using methods that were not environmentally friendly—cutting down trees in the birds' habitats—and highly stressful for the animals. But if he'd really cared about exotic birds, he would have stopped to talk to us and found out more about what we were doing, how our boys had come from a certified breeder, how we'd requested their wings not be clipped so that they could eventually fly free, how much we'd done to give them good, healthy, stimulating lives. He'd also discover that Ken happens to be the only avian veterinarian in this state certified by the American Board of Veterinary Practitioners; he was president of the Association of Avian Veterinarians, which is the international professional organization for bird vets; and he frequently gets invited to speak at international bird conferences—so, to paraphrase Clint Eastwood's character at the end of In the Line of Fire, he knows things about birds. Explaining all that takes time, however, and righteously indignant people rarely seem to want to stick around to hear anything that would complicate matters. And these are the people Ken has to deal with every day without losing his cool and resorting to the kind of belated name-calling I would be so tempted to indulge in.

There is, however, one thing to keep in mind about people who seem perpetually logical and calm: nobody is ever one way through and through, all the time. Think how the logical, unflappable Mr. Spock roiled with violent emotions beneath his glacial exterior. Despite the fact that Ken's daughters joke that their dad is really a robot because his affect remains ever placid, he is abundantly human, and with things he really cares about, he is passionate (which I suppose, in his children's defense, is a word no one wants to hear applied to their own father). When Ken got passionately excited about something, nothing in the world could make me squelch that excitement—even though a part of me knew, with absolute certainty, we were headed for disaster.

What's more—and this is key—he would present seemingly sound reasons why whatever the enterprise was would be a good idea to pursue. After a few weekends flying each bird solo at Level 2 without any overnighters, Ken decided it was time for Boston and Phoenix to fly together. I disagreed; it was not time, it would never be time, certain disaster awaited. Ken, with irritating logic, reasoned that their first duo flight had to happen sometime if it was going to happen at all. The whole *point* of all this was for them to fly together, not for Phoenix to fly while Boston stayed on Ken's shoulder like they were auditioning to be extras in some pirate movie. A delay would not accomplish anything, he asserted.

This is the danger of calm people. Sometimes the people who dash about in wild pursuit of one thing or another know they're behaving irrationally, and they revel in it—thus they're not terribly distraught when things come crashing down later because it isn't a surprise, to them or anyone else. When otherwise rational people get it in their heads to try something crazy, a powerful cognitive dissonance kicks in and they frequently manage to convince themselves—and others—that there's nothing the least bit foolish about this endeavor, that it would, in fact, be crazy *not* to try it.

Back we went to Level 1. No jesses, no backpack perch, a bird on each of Ken's arms, unrestrained, about to be launched. I thought I was going to throw up.

Two things happened when Ken let both of them go at the same time: Phoenix flew straight away from us, fast, with no sign that he had any intention to arc back around, and Boston desperately tried to follow him. Eventually Phoenix had flown so far for so long that Boston got tired or scared or both and dropped out of sight. Only then did Phoenix circle lazily back to us—as though this were just another ordinary flight, an ordinary day—and say, didn't we have some more treats for him?

For the life of me I could not fathom why Phoenix did this. Was he being the bossy older sibling trying to lose his annoying kid brother? Did he resent Boston's taking some of the spotlight from him—did he need to be Top Bird that badly? As for Boston, this time, I was certain it was the end. When we couldn't hear him at first and he wouldn't respond to Ken's calls, I was sure that he'd knocked himself unconscious flying into a tree and was lying on the ground, where some feral cat or weasel-type thing would get him.

Eventually we found him once again in a tree, and as always he'd parked himself there like he never wanted to leave. Boston's instinct when he got scared told him to stay put, even though he was scared precisely because he was stuck in a tree away from us and Phoenix. Getting out of the tree would end the scariness, but he couldn't see that. Unlike the other times he'd parked himself in a tree, however, the night ahead was likely to be an unexpectedly chilly one despite its being mid-spring. Many birds have a surprisingly high tolerance for cold, even birds typically associated with tropical jungles, like macaws, but they have to be acclimated first. Boston wasn't, and Ken knew what that meant.

"You're just gonna stay up there until you die?" Ken asked.

His blunt question went unanswered by Boston, though it sure freaked the hell out of me. It was true, though: if Boston didn't come down soon, the sun would set. Because he wouldn't fly in the dark, he'd stay put—and, not being used to near-freezing temperatures, he would not likely survive the night.

We tried a crazy number of crazy things. Ken tried flinging a rope up to the branch where Boston perched to create a clear way for the bird to climb down. After about a hundred attempts—lassoing an individual branch among dozens is no easy feat—he finally managed to get the right one. Boston stared dumbly at the rope and remained still. At Ken's request I went out and bought some chocolate chip cookies, because whenever the boys saw Ken eating something he clearly enjoyed, they would immediately want to try it themselves. (He wouldn't let them. None of our animals got people food, not even the dog, unless by accident. Ken was adamant about that, having seen far too many obese birds whose people seemed to think their pets were carb loading for a marathon.) Ken called to Boston. Nothing. Ken ignored him, turned his back and walked away, which had always worked with Phoenix. Still nothing. The sun was going down. We were desperate.

In a panic I crouched down beside the travel cage and yelled "Hi!" to Phoenix. The red bird gave me the once-over and said "Hi" back. Ken nodded his head vigorously: this was good; Boston certainly missed his big buddy and might very well be motivated by his voice.

"Hi, Phoenix! Hi! Hi!" I shrieked.

Again Phoenix said "Hi" back, and Boston noticed. He moved around his branch uncertainly, leaning forward a bit in launch pose, thinking twice and hopping to the left or right, then leaning forward again. Clearly he wanted to come down now. Ken, standing atop the car, coaxed him gently.

He came down.

"Quick, get him inside!" I urged. "And be careful!" I added, seeing as how it's a little difficult to climb down from a car safely with a bird on your hand.

He got Boston into the cage, murmuring "Good boy! That was scary, wasn't it." The two macaws huddled together as we drove home, Phoenix now being all big brotherly protective even though he'd been partially responsible for this mess in the first place.

"Well," Ken said quietly once everyone was safe and settled back inside the house. "That wasn't all that bad."

I looked at him the way you look at someone who has just gotten through an ordeal and, because they're through it, they're rationalizing the hell out of it. *Hey, riding out a tornado isn't so bad. I mean, our house is scattered all over the next county, but we're still here. Let's go storm chasing!* Hastily, seeing my look, he continued, "He *did* come down. It was just a matter of getting to where he had a clear path down to me."

"He was there for *hours*. And it's a *tree*. If there were a clear path down, it would be an *elevator*. If it happens again—and it *will* happen again, you *know* it will—it'll be the same thing."

"I'm not giving up on him just yet."

I kind of had given up on him, and Ken knew it. I'd reached a point in my life where I refused to invest too much emotional energy into situations that were guaranteed to be unpleasant with an insufficient payoff in exchange. Spending half the day staring up at a tree trying to get a stubborn bird to come down from it, knowing that a hawk might swoop down on him any minute, knowing that night was coming and with it a potentially lethal chill, knowing that Ken would be devastated if the worst happened—in my view, there could not possibly be enough upside to balance all that anxiety. Getting to watch a bird fly up close and personal wasn't enough for me, even if it was enough for Ken. Ken could create his identity through the macaws: just as with our running group he was Cayenne's person, now he was the bird guy. I couldn't do the same thing. I could care about their welfare, as I would with most any animal, but there wasn't much that was personal about it, no deeper attachment. I could not see myself in them, in terms of qualities I either possessed or desired; I did not see anything recognizable in them at all. They were not my birds, not really, and I had zero expertise other than what I'd picked up from him. Ken obviously loved being the bird guy; I found it hard to think of myself as becoming Mrs. Bird Guy.

But I loved Ken; he loved the macaws. At the very least I'd have to deal with them, tolerate them, learn to get over my frequent fear and occasional loathing. He'd had his heart set on this crazy idea of his (*big mistake*, I wanted to warn him; *a surefire way to get hurt*) that I hated to see him face so many setbacks, and I did try very hard to be supportive, or at least not to make things worse. This, I could see, would be an even bigger challenge for me than flying was for Boston. I could not control these two creatures, but I also could not avoid them, exactly the kind of dilemma I'd hoped to avoid in Act II of my life.

At their best, the macaws were beautiful to look at, amusing to listen to (when they kept the decibel level manageable), and exciting to see fly. Those were enough positives for me; I did not need to cuddle them, did not need them to look adoringly up at me the way the dog did, the way Phoenix did with Ken. I did not want to love them. I was perfectly contented taking care of their basic needs and observing them at a distance. And yet I knew it was not right to have that kind of relationship with them. These were living creatures, after all, not beautiful, high-maintenance toys. I wondered if this was becoming a sort of lesson about what a person decides to love—or whether love is even possible when it isn't up to you to decide.

And that night when we got home and Ken carried the now calm and sleepy pair back down to the basement, I admitted: sometimes, I hated them.

I hated them for obvious reasons. Even without the perils of free flight, they were making our lives hell. They were noisy. They were high-maintenance. They took up all of Ken's free time and much of his disposable income, and he had precious little of either to spare with a taxing job and three kids in college. When I went into the bird room a couple days later to take care of their food and water, which was my responsibility whenever Ken had to get into work extra early, I hit my head on a perch and got tangled in one of the hanging foragers. I looked up and saw them looking back at me, inscrutable as ever, and finally said it out loud: *I hate you.* Quietly, lest they added it to their repertoire.

I also hated the macaws for some less obvious reasons. Hate is frequently more complicated than people think and often reveals a lot about the hater. At times I hated them because they were unpredictable. I don't mean that they were likely to suddenly do something random. There were clearly patterns to their behavior, but I was unable to read these patterns, and even Ken, despite his expertise, could not always do so either. Why was Phoenix sometimes so nice, taking treats from me with almost exaggerated gentleness—like he did that particular morning, as if he understood what I'd just said and wanted to say *Don't hate me, I'm not so bad*—and then other times he'd hang upside down from the ceiling like a bat and spread his wings aggressively and attempt to rip off my ear as I tried to walk by? A lot of things are unpredictable, and I accepted that, but accepting what you can't control is quite different from actively inviting it into your home to be an everyday part of your life—much less nurturing it and encouraging it to engage in even *more* uncontrollable activities.

At the same time, perhaps the very definition of *privilege* is getting to choose the thing that ruins your life. *Something's* going to be the agent of ruin, or so believed the dark-hearted side of me—disease or desire, an oppressive government or a repressive family, the job you're forced to do so you can make your living or the person you believe you can't live without. I reminded myself of this every time I sank into gloom-and-doom mode and got tempted to wish all this had never happened.

That morning, after saying that I hated the macaws, I closed the bird room door behind me and turned to observe them at play. Phoenix held a block of wood in one claw and was turning it into sawdust with his beak while Boston picked up a similar block, threw it down immediately, and tried to join in on Phoenix's block. I reminded myself again: A couple of parrots was hardly a plague. They were noisy, expensive, high-maintenance, and occasionally infuriating, but they weren't *really* going to ruin our lives unless we—unless I—let them. And instead of letting that happen, I needed to find some way to connect to them.

CHAPTER 7

Common Ground

MACAWS LIVE SO MUCH longer than most other pets that everyone who owns one long enough faces the inevitable question of what to do with their bird after they themselves die. More than one of Ken's clients have asked him if they could bequeath their beloved pets to him. More commonly, however, macaws are re-homed not because of owner death but because of owner despair. Many people have no idea what they're in for, and once they find out, they realize they need to get rid of the bird. This is why, in the summer of 2015, the possibility of getting another macaw, a female Military-Scarlet hybrid named Quinn, came our way.

Quinn's owners were a couple whose daughter had been the bird's main caretaker. The daughter was going away to college, however, and the couple felt they'd be too busy to give Quinn the kind of attention she needed. They asked Ken if he'd be interested. Of course he was.

Ken had great hopes that Quinn and I might bond in ways that had yet to happen between me and the boys. In the car on the way to get her, I cautiously harbored similar hopes. If Quinn and I bonded, I would be able to participate more actively and enthusiastically in this whole crazy bird business.

Quinn's people lived in a small town a half hour or so from where we lived, in a beautiful old house they'd clearly done a lot of reno work on. (I was envious, as I watched a lot of HGTV in those days.) Quinn too was a beauty, vividly green and red with pretty bands of color on her wings. As she perched daintily on Ken's arm, he asked if I wanted to try getting her to fly to me. Emboldened, I agreed, held out my arm and called her. She came right to me. I was delighted, but of course I faced the usual question of what I was supposed to do with her next. I didn't have any treats and I didn't dare to touch her, so I just crooned idiotically, "Ohhhh good bird, such a pretty bird."

Quinn gave me the once-over, leaned closer and latched her beak firmly onto my bicep. I once had compartment syndrome in my right forearm, and while I won't say Quinn's bite was in any way comparable to the crushing pain from the hematoma, it was certainly in the same family of pain. This was easily the worst bite I'd ever gotten from a bird—Phoenix's finger nips were nothing to this—but the arm is less sensitive than the hands, so I didn't jump or scream or try to shake her off. I just said, "Whoa" quietly, like you might if a seemingly sweet toddler hurled a heavy toy at you for no reason. Was it an accident, or is there a devil child in your midst?

The owners quickly got Quinn off me and apologized like crazy. I just shrugged. "I've had worse," I said less than honestly. I felt embarrassed more than anything else. Ken was a professional who knew what he was doing around birds, and the family obviously was familiar with handling Quinn. I was once again the outsider, the kid at the pool who can't swim yet and suffers everyone's stares when she's pulled from the water after nearly drowning. As if to underscore this, the teenage daughter took Quinn on her arm and began crooning and ruffling her feathers. I felt like every person who has ever failed spectacularly at something everyone else seems to be doing with ease.

Quinn's bite ended up giving me a week-long bruise. The more important after-effect was that once again I wanted nothing to do with macaws. "I don't understand what I did wrong," I said glumly in the car on the way back home.

Ken shook his head. "You didn't do anything wrong."

I perked up. *So Quinn was just a turd. Well, OK then.*

He went on. "You also didn't do a few things right. You held your arm a little bit away from your body, so Quinn probably wanted to try to get to your shoulder. If you hold your arm with a sharper angle between your forearm and upper arm, she wouldn't do that."

What was I supposed to do, carry a protractor with me from now on so I could make sure my arm was bent at the exact angle to appease a macaw? I'd just as soon opt for the chain mail suit. I mean, who uses protractors anymore?

I thought the unsuccessful first meeting meant that once we brought her home, Quinn and I would be avoiding each other for a while, same as with Phoenix. Quinn, however, had other ideas. She was a very different bird from our boys, raised without other birds around her, and as a result she had become extremely clingy with people. Whenever Ken let her out of her cage in our living room, she would fly immediately to whoever happened to be around. If Ken wasn't there, she flew to me, the only other person available.

The first time it happened, I froze, waiting for another bite. She didn't bite, just perched there on my arm. OK. So I had a bird on my arm. Great. Now what was I supposed to do?

"Ken!" I all but screamed. "Quinn's on me!" OK, maybe I did scream.

"Did she bite you?" he yelled up from the basement.

"No, but ... she's *on* me!"

"That's OK. That's good."

"No it isn't. What do I do?"

"Just keep talking to her. I'll be up in a bit."

I walked slowly around the room, babbling non-stop, nonsensical stuff, all about what a pretty bird she was and now I was going to walk around the room with her, and oh gosh wasn't this nice? I sounded like someone talking to a baby—or else trying to talk a crazy guy out of detonating the bomb strapped to his chest. I would use the same voice in either case, and apparently it was also my bird-talking voice. When Ken finally came back upstairs and took her from me, I exhaled and retreated into another room. No bites, no bruises, but it hardly felt like success.

If it had been only me struggling to get along with Quinn, we might have kept her. But it wasn't only me. The boys were not happy either.

Phoenix and Boston have a very typical big-brother-little-brother relationship. Phoenix constantly pushes Boston around, lunging at him and then acting like it's all in fun. Pretty soon they're wrestling, roughhousing, tumbling around the cage until Ken yells at them. Then it's *tum-te-tum, nothing bad happening here, we're just playing, right, little brother?* And Boston, poor Boston, follows Phoenix around like he's begging for more. That said, Boston can be the bratty kid brother, stealing treats from Phoenix, that kind of thing, but Phoenix was bigger, always would be, and that conferred bullying rights.

And then The Queen entered the picture. The first time Ken placed them on the same perch in the big cage, Phoenix sized her right up, swaggered over, spread his wings and jabbed his beak at her menacingly. Someone clearly needed to show the new bird who was boss around here. Quinn sized *him* up and without a moment's hesitation jabbed right back at him. She was a little smaller than Phoenix but not the least bit intimidated. She charged at him, and Phoenix ... backed off. She pushed her advantage, stepping boldly forward and squawking, wings outstretched, beak poised. Cowed, Phoenix vacated the perch. He hunched on Ken's shoulder as if to hide from the scary girl who was not about to take crap from the likes of him.

I have to admit, we were grinning. "Serves you right, you big bully," Ken chided the big red bird affectionately. "You're in the presence of The Queen."

Phoenix sidled over to a foraging box, picked out a rock—we kept them around the cage for the birds to chew on so that their ever-growing beaks got trimmed—and climbed up to a perch above where Quinn was investigating the water bottle. He inched closer. Ken stepped over toward him. Phoenix looked his most innocent—you could almost read the thought balloon over his feathered noggin, "What? I wasn't going to drop this rock on her, really I wasn't. I just happened to be standing here with a rock in my beak and, oh look, there she is down there below me. What are the odds?"

As for Boston, he kept far away from Quinn at all times. Perhaps he'd observed how badly his big brother was faring and surmised that if Quinn could push even Phoenix around, he himself stood no chance against her. This didn't seem like a bad thing at first; if they stayed apart, there would be no skirmishes. The problem was *where* they stayed apart.

I used to tutor a Tae Kwon Do instructor, a man originally from Korea who had a wealth of experiences and knowledge and wanted to write a book about his life. It was one of those great tutoring gigs in which I learned as much as I taught. At one point he mentioned a Korean metaphor that meant something like "fighting with your back to the river." As he explained it, ancient warriors knew that whenever they saw their enemy positioned in front of an uncrossable body of water like a raging river, they knew they themselves were doomed, because the enemy warriors had nowhere else to go and so were going to fight like crazy. It's a little paradoxical—

usually we think of someone cornered as being one step away from defeat—but it's the same concept as "back against the wall" and I suppose that's the way warfare is around the world. In any case, perhaps Quinn understood this metaphor, or else she was smart enough to realize that standing by the water held a powerful strategic advantage in other ways, because that's exactly where she positioned herself in the bird room.

When Ken went to see them in the evening, he brought both treats and a handheld water bottle, and whereas normally Boston would go for the treats first (water is life and all, but it's just *water*), now he seemed only interested in hydration. Ken was concerned. "I don't think he's drinking at all during the day. He's too afraid of Quinn and she's not letting him by." He tilted the bottle again as Boston guzzled. Ken shook his head. "This isn't working out."

It was not a simple matter of adding more bottles or dishes around the cage. Destructo-Beak a.k.a. Phoenix made it a point to overturn anything that wasn't securely fastened and to mangle anything that was. The one bottle we had was positioned behind a shield of sheet metal to keep him from wrecking it. Yes, we could have created more of these, but that was just a Band-Aid.

Ken had told me what could happen when you brought up a social animal in isolation. Quinn did not know how to interact with other macaws; she had only ever been around people. She was too needy with us and too aggressive toward the boys. Ken had known this might happen, and now that he was sure, there wasn't much we could do but return her to the owners. She was stressing out everyone else in the house, and while Ken could deal with it (and figured I could somehow too), Phoenix and Boston were not faring so well. It was not an easy decision, and we felt terrible about making it. Many times in his career, Ken has shaken his head over some bird owner who somehow failed to grasp the significance of their pet's high-maintenance needs or longevity. It's bad enough that animal shelters are bursting with dogs and cats that people once thought cute but soon tired of; at least there was still a possibility they might find a so-called "forever home." But a macaw might live four or five times as long as a puppy or kitty, which made it even more unlikely that its first owner would be the only one. Transitioning to a new home is stressful on an animal, clearly, and Ken figured it was better to return her to her first home quickly, before she got too accustomed to this one.

Maybe it was my imagination, but Phoenix and Boston seemed a little more relaxed now that The Queen was gone. I felt the same way, and when I looked at them and they back at me, I could swear we were giving each other psychic high-5s—or, in their case, high-4s.

One other thing helped bring me and the macaws together, and it involved another change in the way I defined myself. I was a city girl for many years. Central Park was about as much nature as I could take, and the farmers' market at Union Square was as much agriculture as I could handle. Even though my parents grew a lot of our veggies when I was a kid, for most of my adult life I had no desire to take up this practice. Sticking seeds in dirt didn't sound like much fun, and besides, I had a strong feeling I'd somehow mess it up. For whatever reason, however, the summer after we got our boys, I decided I wanted to grow stuff. I went with the plants I'd heard were easiest to grow: tomatoes, zucchini, green beans, sugar snap peas, lettuce, spinach, and basil. I had surprise successes (the yield on my sugar snaps was ridiculous, almost as ridiculous as my delight in bragging about it) as well as a few disappointments (some fiend chewed my green beans and spinach into lace), but the biggest surprise was how much I loved it. I *loved* sticking seeds in dirt. The second biggest surprise was that this brand new endeavor ultimately ended up being a connection to our macaws.

Ken will tolerate vegetables, but that's about as far as it goes, and there are some types that don't even make tolerance. Suggest a member of the cruciferous family for dinner—broccoli, Brussels sprouts, cauliflower—and you might as well suggest scraping the scum from the shower curtain and serving that up as a side. I maintained that he probably only had these veggies poorly prepared, and that, cooked properly, they could be divine. Mushy, overcooked broccoli is indeed a punishment, but sautéed with lots of garlic, perhaps some Asian seasonings or hot sauce—truly a treat. He disagrees. Strongly.

As for the boys, Boston was a picky eater. He'd clamor for a veggie, hold it in his beak a few seconds and then drop it untouched. It was Phoenix who ended up appreciating my gardening efforts the most. It gave me great delight to hold out a grape tomato to him, watch him take it gently in his beak and roll it around, then grasp one end with a dexterous claw and flip open the top. He would then proceed to scrape out all the insides, carefully, methodically, as if it were a macaw's version of an Oreo cookie, and finally drop the empty skin. He'd do the same with a sugar snap pea, opening it like a clam shell, eating the peas, scraping the insides, and then if it was ripe enough eating the shell too, leaving just the string. He began to see me as the veggie lady, which was fine by me, especially since he took these treats so delicately and consumed them with such obvious enjoyment. There's an intimacy that comes from feeding someone food that you produced, whether it's a mother nursing a baby, a parent making dinner for their family, or yes, even a newbie gardener holding out a little red tomato to a big red bird.

I considered writing the Burpee Seed people to ask which tomatoes they recommended as being the best for parrots. I toyed with delving further into obsessive gardening and creating my own macaw-friendly hybrid. I had no idea how to do that; my resume has zero in the way of botanical research. But at least we had that one connection.

Yet I remained wary. Though we had a common bond in garden vegetables, I still had no desire to interact any further with Phoenix. I could not envision having him perch on my arm the way Boston sometimes did, and petting him was even more unimaginable. It did not help that Phoenix still bit Ken every so often and Ken seemed unable to curb him. As always they were less bites than playful nips. Phoenix clearly wasn't trying to cause harm, but it didn't matter: Ken remained frustrated and I remained distant. Each pleasing moment watching Phoenix munching happily at his veggies would be followed by Phoenix nipping happily at Ken's ear, Ken's exclamations of pain, and my mentally erecting another wall between me and the macaws.

If nothing else, I was at least getting along with them. That was still a far cry from enjoying them, and farther still from feeling anything like love for them. But it was at least a smidge of hope, which I held on to cautiously.

According to Ken, the two of them were getting better at flying, both separately and together. Boston could do longer flights, and when he flew with Phoenix, he kept up for a lot longer before having to land on a rooftop or a tree. More importantly, as far as I was concerned, he was responding more quickly when Ken called him *down* from those rooftops and trees. Sometimes he even had enough sense to fly down on his own without Ken having to coax him. Still, there were incidents. On one drizzly Saturday in early fall, Boston had parked himself in the tree across the street from our yard and had clearly settled into "I'm not budging" stance. The timing was bad; Ken's youngest daughter had a cross-country meet we needed to get to (*What was he thinking flying them so close to the time we had to leave*, I wondered irritably, and then, *What was he thinking flying them at all?*). By the time we got back, it would be dark. If Boston did not come to Ken now, he'd have to get down on his own or else face another overnighter. Frustrated, but still, I could tell, hopeful, Ken headed for the car. He was not going to miss his kid's big event waiting for a crazy bird to show some common sense. He left Phoenix in the outdoor cage in hopes that big brother bird might "call Boston home," the way he had before. Phoenix was indeed squawking on and off (thank goodness the neighbors were easy-going pot smokers who never complained about the noise), but Ken's plan still seemed absurdly hopeful. I didn't say so, however, and tried to take our minds off Boston by cheering raucously for Ken's daughter during her events.

Driving home, darkness falling fast and the rain picking up, we could no longer avoid thinking about Boston. If he was still in the tree, he'd be facing another bad night. It wasn't cold, but few animals would enjoy being soaking wet for many hours. "Wouldn't it be cool if Boston came back on his own? If Phoenix called him back?" Ken said several times.

I murmured something noncommittal each time. Of course it would be cool. It also seemed very unlikely.

We pulled into the garage and got out of the car—slowly, in my case, dreading what was ahead. Ken opened the door to the yard and stared at the outdoor cage. I couldn't see his face, but I could hear something very clearly in his voice: satisfaction. "He's there."

Sure enough, Boston was standing on the cage, and close by on a perch stood Phoenix. Phoenix could have gone inside—the outdoor cage and indoor bird room were connected by a window well that the boys could access via a rope ladder—but he'd stayed out in the rain with his buddy. "Phoenix called him home," Ken added proudly. This particular absurd hope had come true. We were free to continue working on the rest of his absurd hopes for free-flying our boys.

I've never been one to believe in the kinds of positive aphorisms that assert "anything is possible if you just put your mind to it / want it badly enough / try your hardest." That kind of thinking is nonsense, and not even benign nonsense. It's slap-in-the-face nonsense to anyone who has put their mind to something, wanted it so badly it hurt, and tried so hard they thought they might explode—and still failed. Not everything is possible. Some things can never happen. No, as I see it, anything isn't possible—but many things still are, and if you get stuck on one, you'll never see what else is out there. Who knew I'd like running and gardening and living in rural Illinois? But I do. Who knew I'd end up caring for parrots? I did end up doing just that. Would I grow to like caring for parrots? Would those parrots ever free-fly together with complete success? I wasn't sure yet. But I'd done a lot of 180-degree turns in my life, gone from "no way" to "hell yeah" in a great many situations. Perhaps this would be another one.

CHAPTER 8

So This Happened

I N JANUARY 2016 KEN and I flew to the island of Grenada, where Ken was teaching a week-long course at St. George University. As they say, it's a tough job, but someone's got to do it, and that someone got to bring along a guest—me!—for an all-expense-paid vacation in the tropics.

It was our first extended trip away from the boys, and Ken was anxious. I was, too, though part of me was also a wee bit relieved. Finally, a break. Vet school students back home would be caring for them in our absence, and they were eager to get hands-on experience with macaws. Good for them. I myself was eager to get beaks- and claws-off experience in the Caribbean.

Ken and I are not beachy people, me because I grew up on an island and it's tough to wow me with any old stretch of sand and sea, him because he grew up in landlocked USA and has spent most of his life pursuing interests that have nothing to do with sand or sea. As soon as we recovered from the all-day three-plane journey to the island, we eagerly planned on traveling away from the coast and into the lush, green interior. In particular we wanted to hike the Grand Etang National Forest, located in the middle of the island. The bus system in Grenada is pretty good, but the busses don't go that far into the interior. It's questionable whether any vehicles should go there, since the roads are steep, windy, cracked and potholed, and though traffic goes in both directions the roads at their widest can accommodate approximately 1.47 cars. We were determined to hike, however, so we hired a driver and hoped for the best.

"You see way up there? Up there is the best view of the bay." The driver waved his hand toward some buildings on the tall ridge above St. George. "Up there is the prison. The prisoners get the best view in Granada and they get free meals every day. Very nice, isn't it."

Our driver clearly had a good sense of humor, but he also had a somewhat odd sense of what landmarks he felt were necessary to point out to visitors. "Here on the right we have many car dealerships." He pointed to a row of cars. "Isuzus." We murmured appreciatively at the Isuzus.

"Up there is where they blasted the mountainside to get gravel to make houses." We could see the area where he was pointing, stripped away, starkly ugly against the lush greenery. Well, people do need houses, I suppose. We observed the stripped mountain appreciatively.

"Here is a factory. They make flowers."

Ken and I exchanged glances. We had not yet gotten accustomed to the local patois and we weren't quite sure he'd heard him right. Flowers?

The driver sensed our uncertainty. "For baking things."

Ah, *flours*. Still we were confused, since it seemed unlikely that Grenada, the only flat section of which extends for approximately one square meter, has managed to cultivate a tropical variety of wheat grown in terraces like rice paddies. "We get the wheat from outside," the driver continued. Ah, outside. That made sense—sort of. We nodded appreciatively at the factory.

Grenada is a little odd. Its history is like a game of colonial ping-pong between the French and the English. There are a few areas with French names (L'anse aux Epines, where our lodgings were), some with quirky English names (True Blue, location of the university where Ken would be teaching during the week), and some with unknown etymologies (Mount Qua Qua, where we hoped to finish our hike). Because it's in the Caribbean, there are of course tourists—but not really much tourism. Grenada has many fewer chain restaurants and hotels than other vacation getaways. When the cruise ships aren't in and the university hasn't started its term, it looks more like a place where people live their lives than like a tropical fantasy world where visitors wish they could live, believing, as they do, that the people who live there never have to worry about the stressful or the mundane. Grenada is a poor country—the hillsides are dotted with corrugated tin roof shacks, out front of each one a skeletal dog or two—but the residents display a lot of love for and pride in their home. It's not perfect, and they know it. There is poverty, the police are corrupt, and there are massive environmental issues. The island still bristles under the colonial yoke; the Brits won the ping-pong match, and the Queen's face graces all Grenadian currency though the royal family has likely never set foot here. But if we only loved what was perfect we'd love nothing at all.

We made it to Grand Etang and began our hike carrying picnic food and an extra canvas bag, the type given to marathon participants for swag but in this case to be used for catching lizards. Ken was teaching a class on reptiles and nobody at the university thought to supply him with the specimens needed for instruction on handling live critters. He figured if we managed to find some lizards in the forest, we might catch them and bring them back. Iguanas would be ideal, but that was even less likely to happen than lizards. Unfortunately, while we spotted some lizards, they were too fast to catch. A monkey on a railing at the trailhead stared disdainfully at me while he peed, and some frighteningly large caterpillars, big as hot dogs, looked like sons of Mothra in the making, but not being reptiles, they were left alone.

The signpost at the trailhead said that Mount Qua Qua was an hour and a half away. We figured, smug in our ultrarunning prowess, that the estimated time was a wimp's time. Surely we could make the hike a lot faster than that. It didn't take us long to realize our hubris. The trail was shoe-sucking muddy in a lot of places, steep and rocky and rooty in others, and frequently all of those things at once. We came upon stunning views and magnificent plant life, but at some point, filthy with mud, scratched up by branches, and nowhere near the summit, we wimped out and turned back.

So instead of having our lunch at Mount Qua Qua (which frankly I only wanted to see because of its awesome name—say it! it's fun!), we hiked to Grand Etang Lake and ate salami sandwiches and Chips Ahoy cookies in a rain-soaked picnic gazebo by the lake. Some locals were picnicking at another gazebo. We figured they'd probably take one look at us and snicker at the idiotic tourists, tramping around in the mud for no good reason, but they did not. "You hike to Mount Qua Qua?" a teenage girl asked politely. We nodded. "Very muddy," I added unnecessarily. She waved her hand, and it was clear that she'd done the hike herself. "Oh yes, of course."

(Later our driver confirmed that hiking isn't something that only the crazy white people do here. "Yes, it is very fun. You hike a little and slide back down the mud a lot, hike a little, slide a lot. It is a great thing to do!")

In our soggy gazebo, I finished my sandwich and fished around the plastic bag we carried our food in. "We've still got some paper towels left," I said. "We can at least scrape off a little of the mud."

"This isn't how I planned it," Ken said.

I didn't quite register his words, wasn't sure what he was talking about. I put down the mushed up paper towels and looked up to see something entirely unexpected.

He was handing me a box. A ring box.

There was a ring inside. I put it on and said yes.

He had wanted to propose on top of Mount Qua Qua, since I'd been so tickled by the name, and we're both people who would rather be hiking in the woods than dining in a fancy restaurant. Though the moment hadn't gone as planned, it was exactly how it needed to be.

I do not believe that you need to seek the perfect person, the perfect place, the perfect anything. I believe you find the person who will walk through this life with you knowing, as you both do, its contradictions and imperfections. Prisons with views, factories by beaches, mud and a ring. You won't be prepared for everything, and that's OK. That is, perhaps, the point.

"There," the driver said as we went back down the mountain. "That over there is the Coca-Cola factory. They produce the Cokes there."

We nodded and smiled appreciatively. There was so very much to appreciate this day.

CHAPTER 9

The Flying Truck

AFTER SPENDING THE FIRST seventeen years of my life on a small island, I wanted to travel—and I did. A lot of my journeys were solo, as I decided I didn't want to miss out on seeing the world just because I didn't have someone to see it with. This is an admirably bold statement, but I'd be lying if I said traveling alone was all adventure and pleasure. The reasons people are afraid to do it are valid ones. I was lonely in Latvia, friendless in Inverness. I thought about what a big stupid loser I must have looked like, eating alone every night, to the point where I sometimes brought food back to my hotel room instead of going to a restaurant. Even when the experiences were good ones, at times I couldn't help but wish someone were there to enjoy them with me. But here's the thing: even when you travel with someone, it isn't all adventure and pleasure. It's *different*—a new experience, pleasant or otherwise—and with it comes the possibility to learn and grow.

Good stuff, all that.

Yet despite having run a 10K on New Year's Eve in Barcelona and a marathon in Reykjavik (I tended to use running as the basis for my solo travels), I had not traveled much in my own country. Growing up in Hawaii, for all its beautiful weather and scenery, meant limited opportunity to see the other forty-nine states. Later I was lured by lands abroad, not satisfied unless I'd put an ocean between me and my dull daily routines. At the point when I met Ken, I was starting to gain a deep interest in and appreciation for my homeland, specifically for its natural splendor. This was perfect: he, too, wanted to see our forests, deserts, mountains, and lakes. Neither of us was interested in luxury resorts (and—how lucky is this?—neither of us had the money for them either). We wanted to drive, and camp, and explore. We wanted to run trails and hike and kayak and do all manner of outdoorsy stuff. We wanted to do all this together. Perfect.

You can probably figure out the not-so-perfect part.

Many people travel with dogs. I do not know anyone who travels with macaws. Nobody I know knows anyone who travels with macaws. As with any strange idea, this could be because nobody had thought to try it yet and we were among those free-thinking few who dared to be different—or because it's really, really stupid. And as with every strange idea, somebody had to try it for the first time. In the case of an extended road trip with two parrots, that somebody would be us. As Phoenix's flight skills became truly impressive (he graduated to Level 3—the trail where we ran on Thursdays—with literal flying colors) and Boston's improved to the point of at least beyond remedial, Ken grew ambitious to push for the ultimate goal: free flight wherever we happened to be.

He got the idea of buying an old moving truck and turning it into a camper, one specially designed for our particular needs. I thought back to all the cursing, the noise, the heavy things lifted and sometimes dropped on toes, all the madness that accompanied The Building of the Aviary, and I thought, Good Lord, why the *hell* would he want to do *that*? Bad enough our desire to travel was complicated by our small menagerie; worse, in my view, that it would be complicated further by another do-it-yourself venture. But as I watched him search online for potential vehicles, research different materials to be used for the interior, and draw diagrams illustrating his visions, his excitement barely contained by that deceptive ever-placid facade, I felt the familiar tug of emotions. I could not be the one to douse his enthusiasm, no matter how repellent the project was to me.

I am not a do-it-yourself gal. I wish I could be, but I know I'm not. The first piece of some-assembly-required furniture I bought—a simple shelving unit—was so massively frustrating that I decided on the minimalist look so I wouldn't have to assemble anything else. Who needs a bed and a table? That's just clutter. In my defense, the shelving unit was cheap particle board junk, and the only reason I used a hammer instead of a screwdriver as specified was because the holes for the screws did *not* have the proper spiral groove to them. I swear.

It's a little odd that I ended up so unhandy. My parents were big believers in DIY, and I mean DI *all*

Y, every bit. My mother sewed our clothes. My father built our furniture. Granted, a lot of what he made was bulky and awkward and would never be mistaken for something out of Ikea much less anything higher end, but it did what it was supposed to—a flat surface for meals, a few lower flat surfaces for butts around the flat surface for meals, a bigger flat surface for sleeping. What more could you want? Me, I can't get past threading a needle without ending up in tears, and I already told you about hammering the screws. I wish it were otherwise, but the fact remains that other than cooking—I love to eat too much not to have learned at least passable culinary skills— any project involving manual labor will almost certainly provoke an anxiety attack in me. Of course Ken would do almost all of the work and we both knew it, but I would still be there, trying to support him when things went awry, occasionally trying to support heavy objects, ever struggling to stay positive against my true nature.

There is a joke I heard when I lived in New York. Question: Why did God create the goyim? Answer: Because someone has to pay full price. Not a great joke, granted, but I couldn't help thinking of it when Ken found a suitable truck and it came time for him to name a price. He clearly did not want to haggle. But I did. I told myself not to get involved. This was his money and his project and I didn't want to be one of those people whose haggling nature makes their partner squirm. I've been on the other side of things, dined out with people who wanted their drinks comped because they weren't cold enough and their dessert free because it was (not really) their birthday and after all their complaining left a tip so bad the servers might as well have not bothered. People are funny about money, so it's best to accept their quirks and keep quiet. When Ken looked at the dollar figure the dealer gave him and pulled out his checkbook without another word, I handed him a pen and made my face poker-game blank and cringe-free. The truck was bulky, boxy, grimy on the inside and covered with graffiti on the outside, the kind of vehicle you'd cross the street to avoid walking past. And then you might call the cops. And now it was ours.

Ken's first repair mattered little as far as making the truck somewhere we could camp, but it was necessary if we wanted to keep it in our neighborhood. Like many subdivisions, our neighborhood had a lot of persnickety rules that people ignored

99% of the time. One of them dealt with street parking and what was and wasn't allowed. Near as we could figure out given the typically opaque by-law language, you could park a truck like ours on the street so long as it got moved every seventy-two hours. We weren't going to do that. We were going to keep it right where it was until we needed to use it, and we counted on no one caring, since ours wasn't the kind of neighborhood where people complained about stuff much. People kept their yards mostly neat. Nobody played music too loud. Car alarms didn't wake us up in the wee hours, in part because nobody had expensive cars to steal and in part because everyone was in bed at a reasonable hour. To the south were the big new homes by the golf course, to the north was the trailer park; here in the middle, people went to work, came home, did their own thing and minded their own business. That said, the less the truck called attention to itself the better, meaning that the less trashy it looked the better. All it would take was one angry neighbor forced to park down the block on a rainy day, one complaint about that butt-ugly vehicle in front of their door. Therefore, first order of business: paint over the graffiti.

There were a great many orders of business after that: insulation, ventilation, a new door, new flooring, lighting, storage, and a whole lot more, none of which I could offer much help with. For me, DIY should be DETADIY, or "don't even think about doing it yourself." I'm not *completely* mechanically inept; if someone knowledgeable about such things as electronics or computers were to provide clear, well-written instructions for whatever I wanted to do, I could follow them to eventual success. The problem is that clear, well-written instructions on any subject are hard to find. People who know how to do stuff well are often the worst people to explain how to do stuff. It comes easily to them; they don't have to think through every step of a process that's second-nature, so they often neglect to describe the process in full. This was what I experienced when Ken tried to describe the electrical components of the truck. There were inverters and converters, and AC/DC would be there to test the system with their guitars, or something, I had no idea how (though "Highway to Hell" seemed the likeliest choice). In any case, things kept going wrong, the truck had many faulty parts, and it soon became, as I'd feared, a semi-mobile money pit. Our typical Friday evening date nights became a ritual of getting burritos, wolfing them down (we both are fast eaters, Ken because he grew up in a family of fourteen and if you didn't eat fast, you didn't eat; me because, well, I just like food), and then heading over to the Menard's home improvement center to get truck stuff.

After many weeks of this, Ken finally called me outside. "Wanna see it?"

He looked so eager and excited I wanted to throw my arms around him and take him inside and upstairs to our nice comfy bedroom. Instead I nodded enthusiastically and went into the truck.

Ken is not a carpenter or an electrician or a mechanic, so all things considered, he'd done a truly impressive job. He'd made efficient use of the space. Along with a large cage for the boys, there were racks for our kayaks, lots of storage, and a sleeping loft above the truck cab with room for an actual mattress. And yet, as I surveyed the interior, a horrible thought came to me: Good lord, was I on the verge of marrying my *father*? Everything was bulky and hard to get around. Everything was built for someone of his height and strength, not mine. Nothing worked as smoothly as we might have wanted it to. Some very specific childhood memories—uncomfortable chairs, wobbly tables, drawers that screeched and jerked when they were pulled open and took all my strength to push closed—came back to me. I gushed appreciation and praise—and the praise was sincere—but I still felt a little like screws were being hammered into my psyche.

I reminded myself that the truck was going to be for *camping*. It didn't have to be pretty or even comfortable. It was supposed to be functional, which, for the most part, it was. However it happens, in a fancy RV or with just a pack on your back, I like to think that camping can make us rethink our relationship to *stuff*—how much of it we think we need, how much we really do need, how well or poorly we adapt when what we need isn't quite what we get. We often discover that we can do with less than we think. In this case, we would be doing with a *lot* less.

The truck had no shower; we would have to take sponge baths. It had no toilet; we would have to poop and pee in a large bucket with a toilet seat attached, covering the waste each time with cedar shavings that absorbed the odor—as it does for hamsters, I suppose. The interior of the truck could be heated and cooled, but not as well as we might like and certainly not as well as we were used to.

This was a fairly serious concern for our animals. The dog was fine in the cold, but heat could kill her. The boys would have the same problem with heat but could tolerate cold if we gradually got them used to it. They're ancestrally from the tropics, but they are in a sense wearing down coats all the time. Besides, they were born in Michigan where they surely developed some tolerance for extreme cold. The trip we planned was to be in late June, so cold would not be an issue. Heat—lethal heat—most definitely would be.

The heat was only one of many worries, and it increasingly dawned on us just how challenging this trip would be. Well, it dawned on *me*, in any case, and as dawn became the full glare of daylight, I tried to think of how I might voice my concerns to Ken without being a complete downer about the trip. Many parks don't even allow dogs on leash, much less free-flying macaws. Even the parks that claimed to be pet-friendly almost always required leashing at all times. I could just see the park rangers' eyes bugging right out of their heads when they got a load of us. They couldn't know, of course, that Ken had trained them, that he was a bird expert with experience handling macaws. They'd only see newcomers whose presence suggested imminent havoc-wreaking.

They'd have good reason to freak out. Many bird owners *don't* know what they're doing, and untrained pet birds frequently escape into the wild, never to be recovered. Some people think this serves the owners right—how dare they try to keep a wild animal in a cage—but letting a bird go in an environment that isn't its native habitat is a good way to mess with the ecosystem. People think the pet birds will suffer the most—surely they won't be able to feed and fend for themselves in the wild—but even worse is the likelihood that the non-native pet birds will end up beating up on the critters that *do* belong there. This is one way species go extinct, as demonstrated by a long list of examples from around the world. Ken knew all this, of course. He wasn't going to let his birds fly free before he thought they were ready, any more than he'd let the dog off leash if he thought she'd never come back. (In truth Cayenne would enjoy her freedom for about twenty minutes and then miss her milk bone treats and belly rubs too much.) But without knowing Ken's background and the precautions he'd taken to avoid harming anyone, people could think he was some dumbass who wanted to take his birds for a hike in the woods.

Another concern was how other campers might react to our pets, and how our pets might react back. Cayenne was generally a gentle dog, but she'd had some biting incidents when she was sick or when people crowded her travel crate while she was in it. People who think a caged dog is safer to pet than a free-roaming dog are often mistaken. Even a domesticated dog can have a strong fight-or-flight instinct, and when you're in a cage, flight isn't possible. A dog may be far more aggressive on a leash than not, for the same reason: if you can't run away, you've got to put up a good fight. Most people are at least familiar with dogs, so there was a better chance that they'd know how to react to Cayenne. Macaws, on the other hand, are strange to most people. I worried about someone trying to touch the birds or feed them, which would just about guarantee biting. But since most people are a little afraid of their beaks, I worried more about them being loud. As beautiful as our birds are, I doubted people would be forgiving of their decibel level if they got into a screaming match.

As if all this weren't enough, the June trip was to be our honeymoon. The timing was not ideal.

Generally I prefer "hitting 'em where they ain't" and avoiding travel when everyone else is doing it, but June was the only time Ken could get an extended period off work. We joked about how the journey was going to be a test of our marriage—a road trip with pets in a questionable vehicle—but at some level it wasn't really a joke. Someone could end up dead. OK, that's a joke too. But seriously, the trip was seeming like a bad idea to both of us.

With two months to go, Ken said, "Maybe we should rethink this." I agreed, delighted both that he'd said it and that he'd said it first. I did not want to be the wet blanket.

We rethought our plan and figured out a solution. The main part of our trip, covering various National Parks in Arizona and Utah, we'd do with just us, driving in Ken's car rather than the truck, with a combination of camping and motels. When we came back home we'd switch to the truck and head out again immediately with our birds and the dog and camp for a few days at a state park an hour from home. If things went bad we could quickly get back to our own neighborhood. This could be our "practice trip." If this went well we could plan another trip for later in the year. Win-win.

WE GOT MARRIED AT the trailhead where we first met. It was a warm Saturday in mid-June and the guests were as casually dressed as you'll ever see at a wedding, since about half of them were going to run the five-mile course with us after the ceremony. Several dogs were in attendance, including our own Cayenne. The macaws we left at home, for reasons that were obvious even to Ken. I have never believed that a wedding is the bride's day to be the absolute center of the universe, but I did not need this particular day to become Boston's and Phoenix's debutante ball. Some people thought we were nuts for doing our wedding this way, while others were delighted and even came up with additional zany touches. My sister suggested I wear a veil while I ran. A friend sent me a link to a website for a company that made little "flower girl" and "ring bearer" outfits for dogs to wear. We nixed all that. We weren't aiming for a stunt wedding; we simply wanted to do something we enjoyed together. The ceremony itself took two minutes (bad-a-boom bad-a-bing, you're married, congrats), after which we took off for the run with Ken, Cayenne, and me in the lead. Cayenne stayed with us for a couple of miles before disappearing, apparently deciding it was too hot for her. She took a shortcut and met us back at the trailhead, wagging her tail and barking enthusiastically. After the run we all sat on the grass eating barbecue and listening to Ken's daughters sing. They are terrific singers—the youngest has frequent gigs around town with an acoustic guitar accompaniment—so there was our musical entertainment for the day. I even got to do backup vocals for Aerosmith's "Dream On," which happily I didn't screw up. It was simple, inexpensive, and *fun*, which few people I know can say about their wedding day. And, "It was perfect," one of our Buffalo friends told us warmly. He was decked in running shorts with a dress shirt and tie, just enough of a zany touch for the day. "Just perfect."

I looked up at my husband's face, down at our clasped hands, and I agreed.

CHAPTER 10

The Practice Trips

I N THE SUMMER OF 2016, teardrop campers saw a surge of popularity. Several of my friends bought these babies, which were mildly retro and utterly adorable. Compare that to our road trip vehicle, which had no cuteness factor whatsoever—in fact pretty much sucked away all possible cuteness wherever it happened to be. The truck wasn't ugly, per se— once the graffiti was removed, it didn't quite stick out eyesore-like so much—but something about its characterless bulk still made you look, then look sharply away so as not to be caught staring. In the campgrounds where we first tried it out, at a state park about an hour out of town, there were no cute teardrop campers to be found, but there were a lot of massive, expensive-looking RVs, with all the RV bells and whistles and names on the sides as if the campground were a yacht harbor. Nearby us, the "Montana" was so huge and tricked out, it expanded to create several whole separate rooms, one of which might well have been a bowling alley. (Bigger doesn't necessarily mean savvier about camping. The Montana put its trash in a standard trashcan overnight and predictably the raccoons got into it. We kept ours inside, and those bandit-masked critters never bothered us, though perhaps they figured we didn't have any good garbage given our lame-looking lodgings.)

Ours was the only converted moving truck in the park, and, because these things went together, ours were the only parrots. I had the strong feeling many of the families in the park knew each other, camped together all summer long so their kids could play together, and suddenly here comes a suspicious plain white truck into their midst, its occupants clearly not your typical upscale-RV-park family. Ken is not a showy person and has no interest in ever being the center of attention—except when it comes to animals. Whenever we took Boston and Phoenix out in the neighborhood to get them familiar with their environs and the neighbor kids would stop playing and stare and point, I knew Ken loved it. *Loved* it. He loved showing them off and answering questions about them, loved it when an audience gathered around and squealed with delight if one of our boys happened to say "hi!" I didn't mind most of the time, but I can't say I enjoyed it. My instinct whenever I see a stranger nearby—and "nearby" has a rather broad definition in my mind—is to move away quietly but swiftly, all the while willing them to do the same. That was not possible at the campsite.

Even with the macaws on their best behavior, word soon spread, and pretty soon people began walking by our campsite on purpose to get a look at us. We had set up a pop-up canopy tent near the truck for the five of us to sit in to enjoy fresh air. We might as well have made it a circus tent and charged admission.

The macaws were on their best behavior. If anything, the dog was more troublesome, though it wasn't her fault. People kept coming up to the tent to see Boston and Phoenix, and because she was in an enclosed space, Cayenne saw the tent as her territory to defend. She was a sweet, slightly goofy-looking dog but she had a deep, impressive bark, and when she got defensive she could be fairly intimidating. Problem was, many of the people who approached us refused to be intimidated.

Two boys who stopped to talk to Ken and watch the macaws looked like they might be spending the rest of the day with us, completely oblivious to Cayenne barking her fool head off and lunging at them while I tried to keep hold of her collar. "Wow, parrots!" "ARRRRARRRRARRRRR WOOOOOOOF!" "Do they talk?" "WOOOF WOOFWOOFWOOF WOOOOOF!" "I've never seen a parrot before!" "GRRRRRRRR ARRRRRRFFF!" They acted like they were going to hang around forever, and it reached the point where I wanted to start barking at them myself. I don't know, maybe they were used to barky dogs, or maybe it was a tough guy thing, refusing to show fear or even acknowledgement, but in any case it was annoying the hell out of me. A dog that behaves this way is clearly agitated. Unless you're the kind of person who enjoys torturing animals (and their very annoyed owners), you'd best move on. Eventually the boys moved on and the dog settled down, but they were two of a great many.

Though the birds' public behavior was fine, in private, the first night in the truck it was a different story. They were restless. They would not settle down. They clambered all over the cage—rattling the bars as if with a tin cup, like prisoners—all night long. And I mean *all* night. I didn't think it could be possible to get worse sleep camping in a truck on a real mattress than in a tent on the hard ground, but it happened. It was a bit like trying to sleep next to a clothes drier in which you had put a pair of pants and forgotten to take the coins out the pockets. Even Ken couldn't stand it. He's normally one of those annoying people who falls asleep within a minute of closing his eyes and stays that way for six hours, at which point he rises immediately and energetically, whereas I need eight hours and never get it because I spend half the night thinking about all the terrible things that have happened and still could happen in the world. No one in the truck slept well that night. If this became an ongoing thing, travel this way was not going to be possible.

The next morning my mood was foul. I cursed everything in my path, which, given the cramped quarters, was *everything*.

As we finished our breakfast and began packing everything up again, Ken said quietly, "I get the feeling you're not enjoying this."

What could I say? I had been envisioning a certain kind of travel experience, the kind where you bring only what you need and get away from all the nonsense. Get offline, get off-grid, and get *out*. That was all doable for us, but with Boston and Phoenix, our methods for attaining this kind of experience had to be altered drastically. We had little privacy or mobility, and everything we did, we'd have to consider what we'd do with them first. Unless the weather was perfect, requiring no heating or cooling, we could not just camp anywhere; we would have to go to an RV park with hookups to operate A/C or heat. Anything we did without the birds—running, hiking, kayaking, eating in a restaurant—would have to be kept short because they would not be comfortable or safe alone in the truck for long periods of time. If they made too much noise, we might get kicked out of wherever we were camping. And, of course, one or both of them might get lost in an area we were unfamiliar with. In short, the freedom of the open road would be severely restricted, as our pets would dictate everything we could do.

I've always believed the goal of camping is not necessarily ease or relaxation. The idea is to do something different, and to do it with less stuff involved. Yes, I appreciate the irony of buying *new* stuff in the effort to use *less* stuff on your camping trip; nevertheless, it is still a different experience from what you do at home. I was OK with peeing in a pit toilet, OK with cold camp showers, OK with everything being a little dirty all the time, OK with bugs and bug spray, sunscreen and sunburn, OK with a lot of the little annoyances that come from the camp experience, but all that was supposed to go toward a sense of freedom from certain everyday constraints. You couldn't easily shower, so you didn't *have* to shower; that was no longer a necessity. And guess what? You don't die when you don't shower for a couple of days; you don't even notice it that much. I was OK with all that, but for me to actually enjoy it, there needed to be more—or less. Possibly two feathered companions less.

Of course, that wasn't going to happen. Two months later we set off again, this time in the other direction to a state park two hours out of town, where I would be running a 34-mile trail ultra. Camping there the night before the race meant not having to get up insanely early the next morning to drive, for which I was grateful. Bringing the boys along, however, meant that I was unlikely to get any sleep the night before. "Maybe we should leave them at home," Ken suggested neutrally.

I was torn. Ken was going out to the park with me even though he wasn't running the race, so he would essentially waste a whole day waiting around for me to finish. If he brought the boys, he could at least fly them. And this would be another opportunity to get them used to camping before we embarked on The Big Trip. "Well ... I never sleep before a race anyway," I said. This was true; it would hardly make a difference whether I tossed and turned with the boys clanking around the cage or without them.

"Are you really OK bringing them?"

OK seemed like an awfully strong ... word? Term? Acronym that really isn't one? Regardless, I said I was OK.

In the days before the race, it had poured rain. "That's four for four this year," I observed gloomily to Ken the morning of the race, looking out at the soggy campgrounds. All four of the ultras I'd signed up for that year featured non-ideal race weather: one with high winds, two with heat waves, and this one with a pre-race monsoon. Scientists have discovered what causes global climate change, and it's me. The weather during the race itself was supposed to be pretty good—overcast and relatively mild for early September—but there was still the mud to deal with. The pre-race monsoons would make many parts of the trail more suitable for wallowing than running. I picked out my trail shoes with the deepest treads, though it was a little like fighting a forest fire with a coffee mug full of water instead of a shot glass. Cayenne watched me, excited, as I laced up, and then her tail wags slowed with dismay when it became apparent I wasn't taking her (though Ken promised they'd go on a short run together after the race started so they wouldn't get in the racers' way). Before leaving, I looked in on the boys and gave each one a nut treat. They had been quieter at night than they had during the first trip. I still hadn't slept well, as predicted, but I couldn't blame them for that. This was the best way to start a race, I thought, nothing but yourself to rely on. Whether I succeeded or failed was up to me.

The course was on a seventeen-mile loop, with runners signed up for one, two (me), or three loops. The loop wound through forests and fields around a lake, and this being central Illinois, it was mostly flat. It was almost entirely dirt trail, which in this case meant mud trail. The problem with a mud trail isn't that you get dirty. Not big deal to me. I've never been one of those runners who wears a cute running skirt and full make-up to a race. Nothing against those who do. I just figure approximately two minutes into the race I'll already be a sweaty mess, so why bother. No, the problem with mud is that like wind and heat, it makes you work a whole lot harder than you were expecting to. On a dry trail, you put your foot down, push off with it, and move forward. On mud, several different things can happen. You can put your foot down, try to push off, and move backward. Or you can put your foot down, try to push off, and realize that you're losing your shoe. When you secure your shoe and put your other foot down and push off, you finally move forward a little but also sideways a lot, toward the edge of the trail which also happens to be the edge of a ravine, at the bottom of which is a pool of scummy water. You expected to get dirty, but there's fun dirt and then there's pond scum. Not the same.

The upshot was I took a good half-hour longer to complete the first loop than I'd anticipated, and I felt as tired as if I'd already done both loops. It was a good tired, the tiredness that comes from getting through something tough, but the thought of running a second loop made my heart sink like my feet had sunk in the muck. Another loop would transform the good tiredness into pissed-off tiredness. I did not want to go out there again. I so *very badly* did not want to go out there again. What in the world would make me do that? Pride? Determination? The need to uphold my ultra-running badassery?

None of the above. When I reached the start/finish and the scorers recorded my number, I told them I was done. The race director handed me a seventeen-mile finishers medal and told me to help myself to the food. "The barbecue brisket is especially tasty!" he said cheerfully.

Quit a race, get a sandwich. Well, OK then. As I made my way into the tent, I saw three other runners, including a friend, Curt, from my running group, all mud-crusted, all holding medals, all wearing bibs with numbers similar to mine. "Finished my two loops!" Curt joked. We laughed. All four of us had dropped from two to one loop, all four of us wearing the same expression on our faces: disappointment struggling with relief.

For the moment, relief was winning. "No way I was going out there again," Curt said. "I've got a hundred miler coming up. Don't want to screw that up by getting injured." I nodded emphatically. This was a solidly built guy who looks like he could bench press an automobile with me in it. Nobody would say he wasn't badass—nobody who wanted to keep their teeth. I was feeling better already.

When you've dropped from a race, you experience stages of emotion. Relief/disappointment becomes rationalization/regret. The heady exhilaration of the race has waned and you're left overthinking everything, trying to come up with a satisfactory explanation for why you decided to quit. It is, after all, the worst thing you can ever do in running, or so a lot of running culture would have you believe. At first, eating my sandwich, chatting with the other runners, I kept thinking I should have felt worse about my decision. Every time I thought, "If I'd kept going, I'd still be out there right now," every time I looked down at my hands and saw the dirt caked under my fingernails from climbing up those mud hills on all fours, every time I basked in the supreme satisfaction that can come from sitting perfectly still—well, I had a hard time feeling anything but delighted.

Even after I gathered my gear and headed back to the truck, I didn't feel dread at having to explain to Ken why I was back so early. Ken was an ultra runner; he knew how these things went. He hated running in mud even more than I did, so I knew he would sympathize and assure me I'd made a smart decision. When I saw him ahead of me, Cayenne beside him, Boston on one arm, I even felt weirdly happy. It would be all right.

"Hey," I called. He turned, surprised—and anxious. He'd been staring fixedly at a grove of trees, and it occurred to me to wonder where Phoenix might be. "I dropped after one. Where's Phoenix?"

"Somewhere in there." He pointed up—high up, at the tops of the trees. "He's been there for a while. I can hear him but I can't see him. He's *way* in there and I can't get to him."

I stared up into the dense treetops and saw no flash of red among the leaves. I stared down at the mud on my feet, my legs, my hands, felt how tired I was, and yet at that moment I wondered whether I should have kept going for another loop. I wasn't *that* tired. I'd run tougher trails. What had stopped me? And what was stopping Phoenix—*Phoenix*, who had been the star pupil of flight school up until now—from coming back? These two things, my dropping the race and Phoenix being stuck in a tree, had nothing to do with each other, but the combination still felt like a sudden one-two punch of failure.

I wearily went back to the truck to change out of my filthy running clothes and get some more food, taking Boston and Cayenne with me so Ken could search for Phoenix as best as he could, though the trees stood amidst thick brush and it would be nearly impossible for him to get closer without a machete (which, even if we had one with us, I doubt the park rangers would approve of). Reasonably clean, I sat in our canopy tent with dog and bird, willing both to be quiet so curious campers wouldn't come over to check us out, and I waited. Cayenne sniffed at my shoes, perhaps trying to learn where I had gone without her, and Boston swayed back and forth on his perch, clearly agitated by the lack of big brother Phoenix beside him. The longer I waited, the more everything started to feel connected, and not in a good way. Whatever made me think I was so awesome at running ultras? At running at all? At anything at all? Phoenix was Ken's flying ace, and yet here he was pulling a Boston on us. Everything we did lately seemed more humbling than glorious or even fun. Humility was a good thing, I believed, necessary for a healthy perspective in life, but nobody wants to feel mired in mud or stuck in a tree *all* the time.

A shadow, real and not mental, passed over me. I looked up and saw Phoenix, looking subdued but otherwise unharmed, perched on Ken's arm. The look on Ken's face told me that this was one thing, this bird-flying business, that we would not be quitting early.

IN SPITE OF THESE early camping misadventures, I vowed to myself I would never tell Ken the whole thing was a mistake. I would never talk about how much better our lives would have been had he never done this. He *did* do this, all of this, the birds and the truck, and there would be no undoing it. Besides, if not this, something else, I reasoned; better parrots than sports cars, I supposed. So we continued to plan for The Big Trip, this time shooting for November, when heat would not be an issue and there would be fewer people in campsites. Turkey chili looked to be our Thanksgiving meal this year.

But before we took the trip we had planned, and then postponed, and then replanned—The Big Trip that would likely determine once and for all whether the flying truck had been a huge mistake or not—our lives went in a new direction, and we had an entirely new enterprise to judge for huge mistakenness.

CHAPTER 11

The Flying House

THERE WERE PRETTY MUCH only three things I would watch regularly on TV: 1) Baseball, 2) Animal documentaries, and 3) Home improvement shows. Baseball has a long season but once that season is over, it's over; meanwhile, animal documentaries are few and far between. The channels that should be showing this stuff tend to feature instead shows about "rugged" people who live "extreme" lifestyles where nothing all that dramatic happens even though the narrator assures us that death by bear, snake, shark, or avalanche could happen at any moment. That leaves home improvement, which isn't that different from much of the rest of television. Impossibly attractive people are put in made-up situations contrived to produce conflict and rising tension all leading to a happy resolution. In this case the conflict involves things like house-hunting couples who disagree on house styles. Someone always says they like mid-century modern, a dead giveaway that the whole thing is scripted since even the few people who know what that means don't go around talking about it like that.

Yet even the lamest, dullest shows provide nearly endless opportunities for snark. A few examples: Curb appeal. Why is this even a thing? How many times you gonna stand on the curb looking at your house?

- Bathroom size. Why do so many people complain about how small the bathroom is? What are they planning on doing in there, rhythmic gymnastics?

- Bathtubs. Why do people *want* them? You sit there waiting as scalding hot water parboils your body just so you can enjoy the minute and a half that the water is the perfect temperature before you're left sitting in cold dirty water. This is supposed to be fun?

- Subway tiles. Every last designer wants to do the backsplash in subway tiles. Right, because nothing says clean and sanitary like the walls of *a New York City subway station.*

- People who complain about "cookie-cutter houses." You *do* realize you just criticized the way these houses are exactly the same by using *exactly the same phrase* everyone else uses to describe them, right?

- A house that has a perfectly usable kitchen or bathroom but because the cabinets aren't white or Shaker or otherwise don't go with the subway tiles you have planned, you've simply *got* to take a sledgehammer to it and haul everything away. You can't, like, carefully remove it so someone else can use it, no. It's hammer time.

- Many materials can be used for countertops. Granite is only one of these. There is no need to pout because a house doesn't have it, or to shriek with ecstasy because it does. Ditto hardwood floors, stainless steel appliances, and Travertine tiles, which as far as I can tell are just regular tiles with a monastic-sounding name.

Ken found all this mostly amusing, and to his credit, he never asked why I continued to watch these shows when they pissed me off so much. He just rolled with it, assuming there must have been some reason I persisted. The truth is I didn't have a good reason, though I've always had a genuine interest in design, paradoxically because I'm not all that skilled in it. Some people are only interested in things they're good at, and while I'm like that in some respects, there are also things that captivate me precisely because I'm mediocre at them. This mediocrity gives me a deep appreciation for those who truly excel at them. I love the idea of taking an old rundown house and fixing it up. I love the idea, yes, but lack all ability, which is why my first foray into real estate was a condo that didn't even require so much as a coat of paint when I moved in.

Five years later, I entered my second foray into real estate, and it could not have been more different from the first.

You see, while I was yelling at the TV, Ken sat next to me on the couch doing online searches for houses. Well, not houses so much as property—land. He was hoping to find a place within reasonable commuting distance of town where our own backyard could be a Level 1 flight zone. The only way Boston would gain confidence and flight prowess equal to Phoenix's, Ken reasoned, would be for him to fly more, a lot more. That likely meant a lot more incidents in trees. But if those trees were on our own property—because the next closest trees were over a mile away—at least we'd always know where he was, and it would be easier for us to retrieve him. Besides, how cool would it be to be able to fly them whenever we wanted, without having to pack up the car and hope there wouldn't be territorial crows or drone enthusiasts? Our town was surrounded by farmland, flat and open and sparsely populated. Surely we could find a parcel out there that suited our needs.

We looked. All of them were dumps, some not so much fixer-uppers as tear-downers. One place had a foundation so crumbly that the realtor practically sprinted for the door, she could not get out of there fast enough. "What a shame," she said, pointing to the horizontal crack running the length of the basement wall, and then quickly retracting her finger, as if just pointing at it might bring down the whole structure. Many were just old, not charming-old. These were farmhouses, after all, built for function and not form. Ken didn't care. He hardly looked at the houses themselves; he was far more interested in the terrain and the outbuildings. He wanted an aviary, a big one, separate from the house, so pole barns were of far more interest to him than the number of bathrooms and bedrooms. Even the shaky foundation house didn't scare him off right away. As the realtor started her car and waited impatiently for us to get in, Ken was still peering into a shed window, disappointed that its door was locked and we couldn't get a better look inside.

Eventually, we found the one. It was 120 years old on four acres, twenty-five minutes from town and just west of the middle of nowhere, and definitely a dump. Projects! Projects everywhere! There were two front doors, a real one and a fake one, but no kitchen appliances, stainless steel or otherwise. There were holes in the ceiling, cracks in the drywall, and a stain on the master bedroom floor that looked like it might once have been cordoned off by police tape. There was also a terrifying, trashed little room off the master bedroom that locked from the outside—probably a nursery, possibly for a levitating child with a spinning head. There were two outbuildings, a workshop that would become the aviary and a shed that was at the moment mostly full of empty PBR cans. There was a deer pen on the property, part of an old deer farm, which as I understand it is less to produce venison than to sell deer pee to hunters. At the time we saw it, it was thick with brambles that would likely require many hours with a machete. Right behind the house was a pile of junk the previous owners somehow thought would disappear if they moved it behind the house. The pile included an exercise bike, a filthy mattress (there's always a filthy mattress), and *six* TV sets—basically every television these people owned for the past fifty years, dating back to a huge Sears brand the size of a dorm fridge, with big clunky buttons in lieu of a dial or a remote control. It was like the history of television in one broken-down place. The old farmhouse had some cool features, too—nice pocket doors, ornate doorknobs, a beautiful upright piano made in 1904 that had belonged to the original owners—but mostly the place screamed *projects*.

The property was a short sale, which meant no end of runaround and hoop-jumping. It also meant we were getting it for crazy cheap, which further meant it would almost certainly turn out to be a money pit. But it had the acreage we needed to fly our birds and possibly expand our home menagerie, and it would allow us to live a somewhat more off-grid lifestyle—growing more of our own food, using alternative energy sources, making and doing more while buying and consuming less, yeah, all that. It was enormously exciting and absolutely terrifying.

"So this is your revenge on me because I made you watch so much HGTV, right?" I joked to him as soon as we put in our offer.

"Are you having second thoughts?" he asked, searching my face.

Of course I was. Of course we both were. We were both too practical and realistic to imagine the place would be pure joy from start to finish. I cursed a lot just watching TV. Can you imagine the concert of cussing that would accompany my attempts to sand floorboards, strip wallpaper, and dig about a million postholes for fencing in the property? I've screamed myself hoarse when I couldn't get the zipper of my coat back on track.

The funny thing, though, is that I was largely agreeable to this plan. Yes, I had second thoughts, concerns, anxieties, all that, but some days I can barely choose a T-shirt to wear without that happening. In this case, I was deeply drawn to the idea of living in a place where you could look out your window and not see right into your neighbors' window. I craved seclusion, privacy, the ability to be outside and alone and not worried about it but *thrilled* with it, even—especially—at night. I wanted to stand on the earth and not be contained by anything.

Maybe I was ready for another reinvention of myself. All the things I used to enjoy doing when I lived in a major metropolitan area held little interest for me now. Restaurants often seemed overpriced and mediocre, ditto movies and other forms of passive entertainment. Going to stores to buy things particularly repelled me. Granted, I had drastically reduced my disposable income by going freelance and had little money to support an acquisitive nature. Regardless, buying things bored me to a near coma. What you bought usually didn't work out the way you wanted it to or required buying even more boring things. Pass.

I was also at that point where some people start to think about "the kind of world they're leaving their children." Even though I had no children of my own, I had stepchildren whom I loved and parrots who would likely outlive me by several decades, and hopefully several decades left to live myself. So there was all that. Plus it just seemed both necessary and desirable to stop *wasting* so much. Maybe at the point when a certain type of person realizes they have more life behind them than ahead, waste of any type—time, money, resources, life—becomes repellent.

Whatever the reasons, the idea of living semi-off-grid appealed greatly to me, so as soon as we moved I did my best to go crunchy. I began putting everything that could be composted into a compost bin. I learned how to make cheese and yogurt. A friend gave us chickens, six of them, which produced crazy numbers of eggs and even crazier amounts of poop to fertilize the veggie garden. I'm not sure how much better these eggs tasted than store-bought, but they definitely looked different—the yolks almost perfect spheres, thick, and so dark as to be nearly orange. We kept the chickens in the old deer pen and Ken made them a nice coop with a flippy roof so I could easily clean inside. The pen was huge for a half-dozen hens, shaming all other definitions of "free range."

But I'm getting ahead of myself. A lot of things changed in our lives besides our zip code when we moved to the flying house, most of which we were—in retrospect, unsurprisingly—not prepared for at all.

CHAPTER 12

What There Was to See

ALL OUR PLANS TO take our moving-truck-turned-camper to the southwest to see some more National Parks before they got sold to the highest bidder were shoved to the side, next to a very old house that needed crazy amounts of renovation. Sometimes the best thing for your sanity is to rip up filthy carpets and tear down crappy wallpaper, so we armed ourselves with pry bars, paint brushes, and caffeinated beverages.

I wasn't disappointed. I wasn't sure I was in the right frame of mind to appreciate the beauty of

LETITIA L. MOFFITT

America. Our honeymoon trip in the summer had filled me with the requisite awe that comes from seeing just how astonishing the landscape of this country is. But my head had become a muddled, messy place for many days following the 2016 Presidential election, and when you've got a mess to clean up, turning your back on it to look at pretty scenery isn't going to fix anything.

I admit to some very complicated feelings upon realizing that we'd be moving to a very red part of a very blue state. "You'll be the only Democrats in the whole area," a friend who'd grown up around there warned us. "You'll single-handedly be the 'ethnic' population," Ken added privately, since my ancestry is only 50% European. Fine, I thought, since I didn't intend to leave the property except when I wanted to get *out* of the area. This was where I wanted to live, yet I wondered about who else was living here. A lot has been written lately about how people living in small rural towns like the one nearest us—population 200, yet a sign on the main road points to the single-building "business district"— feel forgotten, as though nobody sees them. I get why they feel this way, but I also understand why it's problematic to the point of wrong-headedness.

For starters, living in a small town by itself has never prevented people from voting, marrying, or drinking from whatever public water fountain they want. Still, we'd moved to a part of the world that I would otherwise have driven through without looking. Sometimes you have to ask yourself: What am I not seeing?

The east-facing window of our bedroom looked out onto an almost unbroken view to the horizon. In the early morning, glasses off, half awake, I'd peer blearily out this window and see the earth, open and empty, and in the distance a thin strip of sky on fire. It looked like the apocalypse had finally come. *Great,* I'd think, sinking back into the pillows and blankets, *now people can stop writing trilogies about it.*

Even in the light of day, corrective lenses in place, the view out every window in the house was stark. We were surrounded by farmland, which is many people's idea of a nightmare location (Ken's kids included—when we told them the news they joked about buying us all bib overalls so we could look like farmers together), or at best a quirky lifestyle choice for quirky people like us, since we weren't farmers and intended to use our acreage mainly for the airspace above it to fly our birds. But "the countryside" is more than a lifestyle choice or, if you're less privileged, a place you get stuck in. This was not a landscape of natural splendor like the mountains or a lakeshore. This was not the site of man-made triumph like a great city. It was a place, I began to realize, where you could easily look and not see, because there doesn't seem to be much of anything *to* see. The ground was flat. There was a lot of dirt. Yes, in early winter when we first acquired the house, the snow transformed a bleak landscape into a spectacular scene, the air itself seeming to dance. Then the snow melted and left everything bleaker than before. In a place like this, it's up to you to figure out what there is to see. It takes a different mindset to appreciate emptiness, to find something in not a whole lot of anything—not color, not shape, not movement or change, at least not that can easily be discerned. The place lacked a beautiful view, or an interesting one, but there were big things here: Light. Air. Sky. Vastness. When was the last time I experienced *that*? Now I could do so every day.

The reno started off well, in the early days when we'd just begun shoveling money into this pit. We had a couple of unexpected expenses—the old furnace, for example, which dated back to when phones had rotary dials and TVs had rabbit ears, needed to be replaced. Luckily we discovered this while the weather was still unseasonably warm. Midweek while Ken was at work, I greeted the furnace guy, a jovial man who looked like he played football in high school and still got together with his buddies once in a while to drink beer and reminisce. I showed him the old furnace, and while he did furnace stuff, I went upstairs to Windex the hell out of the windowpanes, which were coated with so many layers of schmutz they might have become archaeological dig sites.

A couple of hours later I heard a vehicle pull up our long gravel driveway. I looked out and saw a pick-up truck with a broken chair in the back. The furnace guy must have called some salvage guys to haul away the old furnace. I watched from the upstairs window as two men got out of the truck, and then I jumped away from the window as if it had suddenly burst into flames.

I was alone in an isolated location and in many ways I don't much resemble the people who live around here. I could tell you what recent events meant to me personally and hope you understand. I could rationalize and justify and defend for great long paragraphs, but the fact remains that when I saw the two men who got out of the truck, I was terrified. They entered the house, bantered briefly with the furnace guy, then got to work hauling out the old furnace. I stood perfectly still, willing them to leave quickly.

"Mrs. Well?"

One of them was calling up the stairs to me. There were three things wrong with those three syllables—it's Ms. not Mrs., it's not pronounced "well," and it's not my name—but I sure as hell wasn't going to point that out. I pasted a smile on my face and skipped down the stairs as though my beau had come to take me to the county fair.

"I seen you got a lot of stuff outside."

He was talking about the piles of junk the last owners had left out there, including the TV sets, which we were having a hard time figuring out how to dispose of properly. He handed me a business card. "I can haul that all away. Just give me a call, I can deal with it."

I beamed delightedly as I took the card, as if he'd handed me a great gift. "Thank you! That would be terrific! We were trying to figure out what to do with all those TVs! Nobody will take them! It's ridiculous!"

As I prattled on I couldn't help noticing that the man had one tooth that I could see. Maybe he had some molars, I don't know, but I wasn't about to ask.

He nodded, encouraged by my enthusiasm. "Also I seen you been taking off the wallpaper. You know the best thing for that? They have these things, steamers, you can rent 'em at U-Rent. Takes the paper off real quick. I did a whole room in just a couple hours."

He explained how the steamer worked, and I listened with a rapt expression on my face. I know about steamers. I also know they aren't necessarily the best way to get off wallpaper because they can damage the wall. But I just nodded and looked fascinated. In the back of my mind I imagined describing this moment to friends, making good use of the term mansplaining.

The guy's buddy appeared—he had on a faded T-shirt with something written on it that I glanced at and then didn't glance at again because I was pretty sure I didn't want to read it. "This is a big house. Looks small on the outside. Didn't think it was going to be this big. Where's the bird?"

The non sequitur threw me until I realized he must have seen the temporary cage we had set up for our macaws. I explained that we'd only kept them here until we finished building the much bigger space they now occupied. He nodded. "What you got?"

"Macaws. Two of them."

He nodded again, more vigorously. "Oh yeah I had two of them once. Blue and golds. How big's the new cage—a whole room?"

Ken had pretty much created a whole other house for them, but I didn't feel the need to go into that. After a bit more cheerful conversation we shook hands, I thanked them for their help, and they drove back out.

I didn't know what to make of this experience. Relief that they were gone mixed with shame at how I'd seen them, the stereotypes I'd affixed, the mean snobbery I'd privately indulged in. What went through my mind during the encounter did not reflect the politeness and civility I showed them. I saw two country boys in a dirty pick-up truck. I was not sure it was a victory that I treated them as though this didn't matter to me when in fact it did matter. I was not sure of many things at that time, but luckily a whole lot of wallpaper needed stripping, and that kind of work may have been what I needed: peeling away the surface layers, exposing what's beneath, and hoping to make it better.

There were many other incidents of people coming to the house to fix stuff, and many of those times our birds became a bridge of sorts. I'm not going to make some gushy statement about how wonderful it is that people can put aside their differences for things like an appreciation of a beautiful animal; that's way too simplistic. At the same time, that connection did happen, again and again. "Do you have falcons?" one of the insulation guys asked. I beamed at him. "No, macaws—good guess, though! Did you hear them?" He'd actually seen the various perches Ken had put in the large field out front, including a step ladder with various PVC pipes attached to it, tree-branch-like. People who drove by would sometimes slow down, probably wondering why the hell we'd put a step ladder out in the middle of a field— what kind of lunatics were living there now? But because the only people who drove by our place likely did so regularly, they must have seen us out there with our birds at some point, so they knew exactly what kind of lunatics we were. Everyone knew us as the crazy bird people. Fine with me. As superficial judgments go, this one was spot on.

CHAPTER 13

Inside and Out

"I LIKE THAT ONE," KEN said.

I looked at the flooring sample he was pointing to. I kept looking.

"You hate it, don't you."

"It's a bit … busy." I peered closer at the label. "'Tiger Stripe.' No wonder you like it. It's got an animal name."

Saturday morning at Home Depot. Ostensibly we were there for the boring but necessary stuff required for more work on our new home: a post-hole digger, a chainsaw, and a lot of cleaning equipment. At some point though we got sucked into browsing for fun designer-y stuff like countertops and backsplashes and flooring. Yes, flooring. You know all those home improvement shows where the couple buys an old house and rips up the carpets and finds beautiful hardwood floors? That didn't happen to us. We ripped up the carpets and found cheap construction-grade planks. The only room that retained some of the original wood floors was the living room, and here one of the previous owners had done something truly bizarre. In the middle of the floor they had cut into the boards and placed a large rectangular plywood inlay. Wood inlays in floors was in fact a design thing back when this house was built, according to various online sources I found, but this was usually done in fancier homes, and the inlays were elaborate and artistic. The plywood clearly had not been original to the house but rather an addition. It was cheap, and as far as artistry, the rectangle had been painted off-white with a black border and a single design element: in three of the four corners, a blobby, amateurishly crafted silhouette of a blackbird.

I cannot emphasize enough how weird this thing was, and I was absolutely dying with curiosity to know what its creator had been thinking. Was it supposed to bring good luck, or was it a symbol of satanic worship? Why only three birds? Why birds at all? Why plywood? Why ruin a decent floor? Was something buried beneath it? Someone? Why—*why*? Ken did not share my curiosity; the poor representations of the birds irked him. Despite the fact that the inlay was in some ways *perfect* for us, he wanted the thing covered up as soon as we could afford to do so after completing other, more critical projects. Hence, tiger-stripe flooring.

Just to stick to a theme, we decided to look for materials that were, or at least loudly claimed to be, eco-friendly—bamboo flooring (sustainable!), recycled glass countertops (repurposing!), all that. It was unbearably precious, I admit. I did not kid myself by imagining that this stuff made us candidates for environmental sainthood, but it at least gave us a way to envision how cool each room will be.

But before we could do anything the least bit cool, we had to complete a whole lot of decidedly non-cool work—namely, cleaning. I'd seen filthier houses than this—I once looked at a house so jam-packed with junk the realtor and I couldn't even get into some of the rooms—and it is true that Ken and I donned gloves and protective masks rather than hazmat suits. All that said, it was still gross work.

Everywhere we turned, there was garbage. Petrified clumps of cat poop and mouse poop littered the kitchen (and given the prevalence of the latter over the former, I surmised that the mice were winning). Inside the workshop we found the bones of a raccoon's paw and outside the rib of a ... something. Possibly someone. In the laundry room I came across all sorts of strange, random items—including, crammed into the back of a broken drawer, a tiny pair of girl's cowboy boots. They looked newish. They reminded me of that six-word Hemingway story: *For sale. Baby shoes. Never worn.*

The true story of the boots might not have been nearly so dramatic as that. Maybe the little girl who owned them simply didn't like them and hid them away. And even though the house seemed to reek of the quiet desperation of the previous inhabitants, it's quite possible their lives were satisfying if slovenly. As a writer I could try to create a fictional narrative about these people, but there are times imagination can't do justice to the truth of our lives. I've taught creative writing students that stories aren't just about what happens; they're about what matters. Well and good, but what about the rest of life? The parts that don't make it into the story, that get left behind?

After we got back from the store, we worked on cleaning for several hours and then took a break—our kind of break. I decided to do a short run around our property. It's a half-mile around the perimeter, but we had yet to get a riding mower at that point and the prairie grasses were still super thick and tall, so I ended up plotting out a quarter-mile loop that was slightly less exhausting to get through. Ken meanwhile decided to get the boys out to free-fly—together. I delayed my run to see how it would go. I think I was holding my breath as he walked out to the middle of our field, a bird on each arm, and let them go.

People used to believe the sky was a dome above the flat circle of earth. Oddly, that's what the world seemed reduced to at that moment, but in a way that felt more about focus than limitation. Suddenly the world was just us and them. Boston and Phoenix took off together and arced around the sky above our land, entwining their flight paths in and out, up and down, first one leading and then the other, twisting, winding, weaving, streaks of brilliant crimson and azure, until they circled around and landed on Ken's arms, first Boston and, close after him, Phoenix. There wasn't much of anywhere else to land, after all, and he was the most familiar thing around. But it was just as he'd always dreamed, and he exclaimed "Good boys!" bursting with elation. I exhaled and began my run with a spring in my step, in part to clear the grasses but also because I just felt springy.

There we were, me high-stepping through the field, the boys above me, circling, soaring, and swooping, and even though my plodding footsteps seemed clumsy and heavy compared to their effortless grace, it felt like sky and earth were mirrors. We were moving, and we were free. The western horizon glowed crimson with the setting sun.

It occurred to me then that whoever lived in this house after us wouldn't know about any of these things we experienced. Who knew what they'd think about us—maybe they'd roll their eyes when they saw our earnest but ultimately half-assed attempts to be eco-conscious, not so different from our wrinkling our noses at the ghastly wallpaper in the bedrooms and the crushed empties in the woodshed left by the people before us. That would be a mistake. Every life is far more than the residue it leaves behind.

THERE WERE GOOD THINGS about being here, many of them unexpected. The dog in particular, though she was getting on in years, loved having her own four acres to romp through. The way she bounded after rabbits, howling with excitement when she picked up their scent, you'd think she was a puppy again—or something even further back in time: a wolf. Luckily she was too old and slow to catch anything, so we didn't have to deal with any unpleasant scenes of carnage, but unluckily she was quite deaf and thus impossible to call in when the day was done. One night in late spring, she stayed out well after sunset, willfully ignoring our attempts to get her attention in favor of cavorting through the field. When one of those crazy storms materialized out of nowhere, the winds kicked up and the rain poured down, she remained unfazed. Maybe she'd decided to enact that scene where King Lear rages at the storm on the heath, too dimwitted to realize she shouldn't emulate a fictional madman in a situation involving lightning.

Eventually she came inside looking like she'd been through the rinse cycle a couple of times. She shook herself off on the rug and curled up contentedly to snooze. She was a domesticated pet, after all, and not truly wild, though living out here, it was becoming easier to see the streaks of wildness in her.

Farmland is not truly wild, of course. Rural areas are just as worked over by the human hand as urban ones. But it was less easy to be in denial about the forces of wildness out here than in the city, where critters going through the trash and weeds poking up through cracks in the sidewalk were occasional annoyances that could be dealt with by purchasing appropriate products. The fewer buildings, cars, and people per square foot, the harder it becomes to ignore these kinds of unexpected encroachments.

Even the aspects of nature that we had some degree of control over—the plants we grew, the animals we raised—were echoes of the natural world. We had six chickens, which ate and drank and pooped and clucked, and whenever I appeared at their gate they came racing toward me doing that funny chicken dash. Watching them, Ken said they were more like dinosaurs than any other birds he'd seen, and while I didn't know enough about dinosaurs or birds to make that judgment, I did know that these creatures were the same as the ones who gave us the Styrofoam-and-plastic-wrapped parts thawing in the fridge. This wasn't enough just yet to make me give up meat, but it was a new experience for me, as it would be for many people, to be see what the creatures I ate looked like before they were deemed food and not life.

Elsewhere on our property, there were several mulberry trees that had already dropped a tarry mess of fruit before we got the bright idea to harvest them. Mulberries look and taste a bit like raspberries except each mulberry has a tiny stem that is nearly impossible to extract without a lot of frustration. Luckily, thanks to a visit to Dr. Google, I learned these stems were digestible. Mulberry muffins, mulberry jam, mulberry juice, mulberry soda, frozen mulberries in smoothies, fresh mulberries on yogurt—for a while we were the fruit version of Bubba Gump. Sometimes we put Boston and Phoenix in a tree and let them forage naturally, and after some initial hesitation they became quite good at plucking off berries and gulping them down whole.

When I told my mother about our berry trees, she suggested we get some silkworms. "They eat mulberry leaves," she informed me. "You can make silk." This was a surprising suggestion coming from her, given that she'd been initially dubious about my neo-granola lifestyle. All this stuff—washing dishes by hand, growing food, making instead of buying—she'd had to do for real, not as a lifestyle choice, so she found it odd that anyone would want to go back to all that. Still, she supported me through every lifestyle choice I ever made, this one included, so I listened attentively to her silkworm proposal even though that was never going to happen. ("Do you have room for a horse?" she added. In addition to growing our own food and making our own clothing, apparently we were to eschew motor vehicles for equine transportation.)

We also discovered some slender fingers of asparagus growing—not wild asparagus, a cultivated variety, no doubt a remnant from the previous owner's vegetable garden, but weird and surprising nonetheless. Even more surprising was what happened when we decided to let some of it keep growing, just to see what would happen. Seasoned gardeners would no doubt laugh at us, but I had no idea what asparagus looks like coming out of the earth—and how quickly a patch of it can turn into a grove of small trees.

There is a will, a determination, that living things have. We may call it wildness if it's something that surprises us, something we can't control, but maybe it's just part of being alive.

Our macaws were born and bred in captivity, so they aren't really wild, but they also aren't domesticated species. This is a point of controversy to some people who think it's wrong to have them as pets. Of course, some people think it's wrong to have *any* animal as a pet. I could see why they'd think this, and when you consider the mistreatment of animals around the world as well as the way pet owners are often woefully unprepared and filled with more misinformation than knowledge about caring for their animals—well, sometimes I wondered if they were right. Yes, animals in captivity frequently live much longer, healthier lives than those in "the wild," but that brings up the question: what kind of life is it? Had we given our pets a good life, one that would allow them to do what they were born to do—fly free—or were we simply indulging ourselves?

Maybe that was the wrong way to look at all this. When we cared for our animals, we automatically thought of them as *animals*—separate from ourselves, even though we were a subset thereof. But we can't really separate ourselves from "the natural world." Our land was neither completely wild nor completely "manmade." No square foot of this planet has not been affected by human activity; likewise, no aspect of our own lives has not been shaped by nature. "Coexist," I was starting to see, is not just a groovy bumper sticker slogan; it's a smart, sensible, ethical way to live. Humans and other animals have coexisted for a long time, in a number of different ways, for better and worse. I couldn't speak to every one of those different ways; I was still working out the few I dealt with personally. Perhaps it is just an indulgence to watch two beautiful birds fly around you, vivid colors streaking through space, iridescent in the sunlight. Perhaps it's wishful thinking when you see the joy of movement in those stunning creatures, a mirror of the joy you feel beholding that sight. But I think it is more than that.

One night just after sunset I went out to bring the dog in and stopped a few feet from the house, looking slowly around me. The fields were glittering with fireflies. I'd seen fireflies before, of course, but it's one thing to see them in your backyard in the burbs and quite another to see them when your backyard is the size of a couple of football fields which blend seamlessly with all the other backyards in the area and cumulatively stretch clear to the horizon. It was as if half the Milky Way had fallen to earth and decided to stick around awhile to see whether this place was any good. I figured if I saw them the next night, I'd know they decided in our favor.

So fireflies are stars, chickens are dinosaurs, the dog is a wolf, and asparagus becomes a forest. I wondered about what wildness might still be inside us all, Ken and me, Boston and Phoenix, whether it was beautiful or frightening or both, and how it might reveal itself in unexpected ways.

THOSE WERE SOME OF the good times. Then there were other times.

We were just so bad at all things reno-related. Everything we got done was half-assed. Everything else didn't get done. And there was one problem after another after another. The roof leaked. The kitchen sink leaked. A portion of ceiling plaster in the laundry room crashed to the floor for no particular reason. There were mice. Mice are cute until you find one in your sock drawer; then they are the enemy. At different times we had no heat, no hot water, no water at all, only one working toilet with a tank that needed to be filled manually, dead-thing smells wafting up from the crawl space, and live things crawling in the living space. And of course, projects. Every square foot a project.

I tried to convince myself that at least some of the projects we did were OK. Sometimes the white-washed walls of the kitchen looked cool and appropriately rustic. Other times they looked like a bad paint job. Ditto the concrete countertops—cool-and-funky one minute, a blobby grey mess the next. Without exception, everything looked amateur-ish, which made sense given that we were, in fact, amateurs. But that wasn't how renovations turned out on those stupid TV shows. I stopped watching HGTV shortly after we moved.

The upside, of sorts, was that with *so* many problems to deal with, some of them didn't faze us. Garbage pickup was only twice a month. Shrug. We could compost and recycle. We had no dishwasher. Also a shrug. It was usually only the two of us and we used very few dishes. The water in the washing machine was extremely hard, even with softener, and our clothes came out stiff and wrinkled into mountain ranges. Still shrugging. I work from home;

who needs to look neatly pressed? Ken works with the public, but his job also involves getting animal hair et cetera all over him, so neatly pressed hardly matters there either. Yes, I was rationalizing, and I was actually more successful at it than Ken was. He was starting to wonder what we'd gotten into, and why. I refused to ask those questions. We knew the answers already. The goal now was to deal with what we'd gotten into, and at that point I firmly believed we could deal with it. I still strived to believe that what we'd gained would be greater than what we lost.

CHAPTER 14

What Got Lost

Part 1, June 2017

A MAROON STATION WAGON WAS making its way slowly down the long driveway toward our house. I walked as fast as I could without looking too alarming about it, still clutching the eggs I'd just gathered from our chickens.

Maybe. Maybe they'd found her and were bringing her home.

"Hello! My husband used to live in this house twenty years ago! We live in Iowa now but we're passing through the area and he wanted to see the old place again."

She looked so nice and sweet, it was hard to believe she could have been so cruel. Of course she wasn't trying to be cruel; she had no idea Cayenne was missing, had disappeared just two days prior, so I put on my Good Country Folk face, shifted the eggs to my left hand and offered her my right. She introduced herself, and her teenage daughter still in the car, while another car pulled up and a man, presumably the husband, got out. A third car pulled in behind his, with a teenage boy at the wheel. Four people, three cars: 'merica.

More handshaking, and smiles, and general cheerfulness. "How do you like living here?"

Right at this moment, I couldn't be more miserable, but thanks for asking. "It's great! We love it!"

They told me a little about the history of the house, what they'd done with it, what the owners after them had done, or not done, since most of the deterioration and decay that we inherited had happened during the interim when that other family ran out of money and split apart. "They tried," the husband said with a sad smile.

ANOTHER CAR PULLED UP the drive in the evening, this one going all the way around to the back of the house where we park our own cars, as though the driver was one of the family.

I went out to meet him, a man who looked a little like Fred Gwynne, with just as jovial a demeanor as Herman Munster but no cracked forehead. "Hello there! I'm your neighbor." He pointed south, to the farm nearly a mile away. "Are you the owner of..."

A dog. Yes. Yes, we have a dog—or had one, up until two days ago. She's been missing. Just wandered off—at least we think. I'm talking about the dog you have in your car right now, correct? Yes. Thank you. Bless you, Fred Gwynne's rural Illinois kid brother.

"... a couple of parrots?"

It took me a blink or two to slap on the GCF face again and exclaim "Yes, yes we do!" and enthusiastically answer his questions about our macaws, which he had just seen flying over the soybean fields. Their flight prowess had become so strong that during the long days of summer, Ken had felt comfortable letting them fly around unsupervised while he was at work. He'd have me let them out in the afternoon with plenty enough time for him to gather them back before sunset once he got home. Phoenix had even taken to waiting on one of the perches in the field around the time Ken usually returned from work and flying around his car when it turned up the driveway—much the way a dog might happily greet its person.

I apologized profusely for any noise they were making—a large part of the reason we moved out here was so that we could do our own thing without bothering people—or people bothering us. Our neighbor waved the apology aside—there was no bother at all.

His name was Floyd, or Lloyd, or maybe it was something else I didn't catch and I just had the stereotypical mindset that people who live out here have names like Floyd or Lloyd. He had seen the flier we'd put in his mailbox, about our dog, and he asked about her. I told him where things stood, which was still. We had no leads.

He shook his head. "I'm so sorry. Hope you find her soon."

Me too, Floyd Gwynne. Me too.

AN HOUR LATER, YET another visit, this time a young couple in a go-cart-looking vehicle in the now familiar green-and-yellow of John Deere. There was no raising of hopes this time; clearly they did not have a dog in the go-cart.

"Hello! We're your neighbors!" They pointed north, to the farm nearly a mile away in that direction. "Are those birds yours? They're beautiful!"

More introductions, more pleasant conversation, more curious questions about the birds, more well-wishes about our dog, since they got the flier too but had no information either. They, too, assured us our macaws were not bothering anyone. "They're just so cool," the man said, and his wife nodded vigorously. "It must be amazing to get to see them fly all the time." They were so enthusiastic, I found myself telling them to feel free to come on over to watch them fly whenever they wanted, even though that was not something I wanted.

"I think you'll like living here," the young woman said as they waved their good-byes. "This is a great place to live."

I agreed with her, and up until a few days ago my agreement would have been sincere. Now my words felt a little hollow. I said them anyway, all of us smiling, gazing around at the open fields and the great big sky.

Move to the country, think you're getting solitude and privacy, discover you're getting something
else entirely. The vast spaces you so longed for have
turned out to be a nightmare when you think about
what you've lost; meanwhile the neighbors are stopping by like it's some kind of summer block party
even though the block is a mile long and there are
only two houses on it. That's not to say these vis-
its were unwelcome. Sometimes solitude and privacy are exactly what you don't need. Regardless, I
kept waiting, watching, to see who came down our
driveway next.

THE DAY CAYENNE HAD disappeared, we looked for
hours. We covered every square foot of our property, checked the shed, the wood pile, throughout
the workshop, in the crawl space, in the attic, in every single room and in places she couldn't possibly
be but we were damn well going to look anyway.
We drove around the farmlands and in the nearby
town, taking turns doing so, with one of us waiting back at home in case she returned. We looked in
terrible places, checking the ditches on the side of
the roads in case she'd gotten hit, scanning across

the fields to see if vultures might be gathering in one particular spot. We saw nothing at all.

She had seemed fine that day. She was an old dog, sure, but not one to go wandering off without coming back. The last I'd seen of her, she was contentedly roaming our field, her frosted red back bright among the drab grasses.

This was one of the worst days of my life, and certainly the worst day of my life with Ken. "Fifteen years," he said quietly, staring out into the dark field that night. "Is this how it ends?"

I couldn't answer him. I was heartsick with worry and sorrow, but there was something else as well: I blamed him. Not a day before I'd told him Cayenne was getting awfully close to the road, and maybe we should stop letting her roam around the property all day. He'd waved that concern aside; I was definitely the more pessimistic of the two of us, the eternal worrier, and anyway he was the animal expert. He had figured Cayenne would be fine. I had not figured this. Now she was gone.

It went even further than that, though: if we had not moved out here, we would not have lost her. And the only reason we were here was because of him—and *them*. If we had to lose a pet, I would think bitterly in the following weeks, why did it have to be the one I cared about?

I did not say these things. I knew, even in my emotional turmoil, that if I said them, I would regret it forever. The dog might well be lost; I did not want to also lose my marriage.

Part 2, August 2017

IT'S A CRUEL TRICK of the calendar that the minute it's "officially" summer, the days start getting shorter. Even though this happens every year, it can still be dismaying anew the moment you realize night is falling just a tad bit sooner than it did last week. It's the sun's big tease: *you enjoy all this daylight, do you? Don't get used to it. Australia needs me too.*

I had been thinking about the things we love despite knowing they'll all too soon be gone. (I'm *great* at parties. Having too much fun? Let's discuss loss and misery!) I don't actually relish thinking grim thoughts all the time, but I have a hard time avoiding it. The trick is in the balance, something I strive for but don't always achieve. More often there's the face I show the public and the one I bash into my pillow at night when I can't sleep for all the suckiness in the world. Sometimes, as happened the summer we lost Cayenne, the two faces come close to merging at the worst moments.

The daughter of our friends asked Ken if he knew of any volunteer opportunities for kids during the summer that involved working with animals. Unfortunately most such opportunities require volunteers to be at least high-school age, and she was quite a bit younger than that. Ken suggested she might volunteer *here*, at our place, helping to care for our small menagerie. In truth we don't have more "pets" than most rural people do, and the ones we have are not all that unusual. It's just that Ken's job at the university clinic also entails being the official vet for a nearby zoo, and the affection with which he talks about exotic animals prompts our friends to ask questions like how big our lemur habitat will be and whether the wombats will get along with the capybara. At last count we had a half dozen chickens, two turtles, and two macaws. A couple months ago, there had also been a dog.

This seemed sufficiently intriguing for our friends' daughter, so her father dropped her off one weekend and Ken and I showed her around and described her volunteer duties. I wasn't sure how this would go. It was quite possible that any desire she had to pursue a career relating to animals would vanish once she started scooping poop and plunging her hand into a big bag of dried mealworms. Then she might turn her attention from Ken to me and focus on her career as a novelist. We've pretty much got the monopoly on cool jobs, as far as our friends' kids are concerned, as many of them have expressed an interest in working with animals and nearly all of them, certainly all the girls, want to write books. At least a couple wanted to combine the two areas and write books about animals. At the moment, though, animals alone were front and center.

To her credit, she did not mind the yuckier aspects of animal care. She eagerly hunted for rotting pieces of wood that might be filled with tasty crawly things for the turtles. "I don't care if I get my hands dirty," she asserted, picking up a food dish caked with crud, "just as long as I can wash them later."

Some of the activities we had lined up were not only unglamorous but decidedly dull, involving wrapping small pellets in scraps of paper to be hidden around the macaws' room for them to seek out as foraging. Take a pellet, put it in the center of a square of paper, and twist the ends of the paper closed. Now do that another ninety-nine times. I probably wouldn't have made her do this except her parents insisted she was there to volunteer, not to play, and as such she needed to be useful. She did offer to help us work on our fixer-upper, which would have been *totally* be useful, but that might have been going a bit too far.

And it wasn't all drudgery either. We had not yet managed to differentiate between our six hens, so one of her activities was to observe them and see if she could tell them apart, as well as to log their behaviors and get them used to being handled by people. This last item, I cautioned her, might take time; they were not at all aggressive and would not peck at her, but they were not used to being touched and so would likely be skittish at first. These tasks she took on with admirable persistence. She would crouch and slowly bring her hand toward a chicken, not getting discouraged if it darted away, simply waiting a bit and trying again.

I was impressed—and uneasy. It occurred to me that there was something a little dishonest in my instructions to her—or, worse, devious. One of the reasons we needed them to get used to being handled was because one day they'd be too old to lay eggs, and then we would have to catch them in as non-stressful a way as possible, end their lives as humanely as we could, and eat them.

Maybe that sounds horrible, raising an animal like a pet only to kill and consume it. I could give you the standard justification: practically speaking, they are a potential source of food, and food should not be wasted, especially food that checks off all the ethical-and-local boxes. Far better to know where your food is coming from, and to know that the animal had a good life, than otherwise. What's more, if I felt just as horrified, I'd be a hypocrite. If I couldn't deal with seeing one of our chickens killed (which would be Ken's job) and then plucking and gutting and all that (which would be mine, since it was probably *way* out of the bounds of what we could have a volunteer do)—if I couldn't handle that, as any vegetarian understands, I shouldn't eat animals at all. It would be so easy to dissociate, to say *this is an animal and it's alive; it has nothing to do with breaded and fried patties on a bun or grilled chopped morsels in a taco.* But that's a lie. These were animals and right now they were alive, but they wouldn't be some day, and I'd have to deal with it one way or another.

I wasn't about to go into all that with a ten-year-old, however, and in truth, there was only one thing I wanted to say to her as she ran a gentle hand over a feathered back: *Don't get attached. Don't care for them too much.* But that's foolish advice, because no one would listen to it, ever. Many people would argue that no one *should* listen to it—would insist, instead, that we are supposed to get attached to things, desperately, and love them without reserve, even though doing so risks being absolutely destroyed when they're gone. I don't know that I agree, or at least I didn't at that moment. At that moment, the pain of loss—because up until a couple months ago, there had been a dog—was such that I wished I could take that advice and stick to it. Don't get attached. Don't care too much. Stay distant, reserved. Don't put yourself in a position where you find yourself holding on to things that you can't imagine being without—because one day you might be without them.

Of course I neither gave nor took that advice, never have given or taken it, probably never will.

The fliers, website posts, and everything else we did yielded nothing. We never saw Cayenne again.

The only thing that made the loss hurt marginally less was that I never told Ken I thought it was his fault. Once I put aside my own despair, I no longer thought that, and I realized he was suffering a lot worse than I was. He already blamed himself. This dog had been his companion for a decade and a half. His kids had grown up with her. She had come with him after his divorce and, as he put it, had given him someone to come home to in those days. She was his running buddy, the beloved Buffalo dog. She had been part of our story, had been there on our wedding day. We had both figured on there being a sad day in the near future when we had to say good bye to her. Now that day would never come, and we felt so much worse because of it.

Eventually I was able to talk about her, laugh about the funny things she did, that sound of disappointment she made when she wanted to go out running but we were busy, the goofy look on her face when she raced ahead of us on a trail and then turned to wait for us to catch up, the disgusting habit she had of eating her own poop and vomit, the weird way she'd twitch and yelp in her sleep. I remembered, enviously, how she was largely unfazed by the macaws, even when they tried to tease her by dropping things on her or pooping on her or, in Phoenix's case, sneaking over to nip her on the tail. I wanted us to start remembering the good stuff, instead of wondering if she was still alive and being cared for by good people, or if she'd died relatively quickly and painlessly or ... something else. I wanted to make it clear that I did *not* blame him, though I'd felt that way at first, and that I understood how much harder this was for him.

My attempts to make things better failed. He still could not talk about it, couldn't reminisce about the good times without pain.

Even to this day, whenever we go on trail runs, there will be times when I know we're both thinking the same thing: Cayenne would have loved this. I know Ken would be looking for her, always secretly hope that she'd come trotting up alongside him like she used to, with that goofy grin on her face, so excited to be running free with us again.

CHAPTER 15

What We Gained

WE INHERITED A NEW macaw in September 2017 from two of Ken's clients who were getting too old to care for their high-maintenance pet. I was wary after the Quinn debacle, but Ken assured me that this bird was quite different from The Queen. He was a green-wing macaw, like Phoenix, but gentle, unlike Phoenix, and mature, unlike Quinn. He was 25 years old and his name was Fred. This didn't quite fit the two-syllable city-name theme we started with our boys, but we could pretend that Fred stood for Fredericksburg, which could be altered to "Fredericksbird," which could be shortened to Fred Bird. (Ken was a St. Louis Cardinals fan, so this worked nicely.) The transition to new people had likely been traumatic enough; no need to further torment him with a new name, as appealing as it would be to have a parrot named Vegas or Raleigh.

Fred was understandably a bit freaked out at first by his new environment. Ken was the only familiar element, and Ken was Fred's vet, which is a little like a child being adopted by their dentist or the principal of their school. Initially we kept him separate from our boys, but gradually we began putting the three together in hopes that they'd all get along and perhaps even be buddies one day. They're social animals, and in the long run having other birds around him would, in theory, give him a better life. The transition, however, would be tough.

In an odd sense, this would not be the first time Phoenix and Boston met Fred. As mentioned, Phoenix and Boston had gotten grafted feathers in their early days so that they could fledge despite their clipped wings. Boston had gotten his from a blue-and-gold named Webster, and Phoenix's feathers had come from none other than Fred himself. In other words, part of Fred had briefly been part of

Phoenix, and Phoenix owed him big time for helping him fly. Of course, there was no way for any of them to know this, so we had to hope they would all get along anyway.

Surprisingly, Fred did not seem perturbed by his two new roommates. When Phoenix first approached Fred, stretching his body out to look bigger and fake-lunging at him, Fred held his ground. Didn't snap at Phoenix, didn't squawk in anger or fear, just kind of stared him down. I liked to imagine him mentally rolling his eyes and thinking *Oh brother, look who thinks he's Mr. Big Shot. Give the old man some room, will ya, kid?*

Still Phoenix needed to assert his Top Bird status. He tried again: marching over to Fred, he leaned over and said, "Buh-bye."

This was something Ken would say when one of the boys was in a tree and not coming down right away. If they thought Ken was going away to do fun stuff that didn't include them, that was often enough to bring them over to him. In this case, however, Phoenix clearly meant it as, Go away.

Fred wasn't going anywhere. He straightened up and spread open his wings, a trick his former people had taught him. "Get 'em up!" he called, which was what his people said to get him to perform (though Fred's enunciation wasn't the greatest, and it sounded more like "aggamoo!" to me). This was just a trick, but it's also something macaws do as a sign of aggression, and Phoenix definitely took it as such. This was war.

Over the next several weeks, Phoenix and occasionally even Boston bombarded Fred with their full arsenal of words they associated with wrongdoing.

"No!"

"Drop it!"

"No!"

"Let go!"

"No!"

"NO!"

Nothing doing. Fred wasn't Quinn; he wasn't hoarding the water in hopes of dehydrating the other two to death, but he wasn't a pushover either. He would fight back if he needed to, stretching out his body to look bigger and jabbing his beak to parry whichever beak was jabbing toward him. Further unlike Quinn, much to my relief, he displayed none of these aggressive behaviors toward me, and he was fast becoming my favorite.

When Ken told his colleagues about the things Boston and Phoenix were saying to Fred, they laughed, but some of them were also skeptical. Intelligence in non-human animals has been an enormous issue for a long time, with facility for language being one key aspect of the debate. Were those famous gorillas who were taught sign language really using sign language to express themselves, or were they merely performing a set of behaviors they knew they were being encouraged to perform? Did Alex, Irene Pepperberg's legendary talking parrot, actually understand the things he was saying, or was it just clever mimicry? Obviously I can't answer questions like this at all, and even Ken could only quote from studies he'd read, though he clearly sided with those who asserted that the gorillas, the parrot, and many other animals are capable of language the way humans are. This side of the debate bristles at criticism that they are wishfully anthropomorphizing the subjects of the studies, and it irks them to hear animals characterized as stupid and mindless despite what they see as strong evidence to the contrary. The only evidence I can contribute is anecdotal, but for what it's worth, seeing and hearing our three guys interact, I find it impossible not to believe they could use language the way we do. In their early days together, Boston and Phoenix only ever said words and phrases associated with negatives when Fred was around. Later on, as everyone started to get along better, that changed. If they were only imitating what Ken said, or if they processed words the way a dog does—as prompts to take certain actions—they would not have selected certain of these prompts to use on each other in appropriate situations. Take it for what you will. I take it for a sign of linguistic capability and intelligence—as well as a sign that macaws too understand the power of words as weapons.

Like Boston and Phoenix, Fred wasn't much of a talker. He said "hi" a lot, though curiously he made it sound like a question: "hi?" Many of the other things he said weren't simply random repetitions of his people or us but rather linked to actions he did or wanted done. If we gave him a stick to play with, he would clasp it in a claw, wave it jerkily up and down and say, "Want this?" (The first time he did this when Phoenix was standing next to him, Phoenix leaned away slightly and stared, about as perfect a "WTF?" look as there could be.) If we gave Fred one of his favorite treats—a walnut, perhaps, or a piece of banana—he would say "Mmmm" and "Is that good?" Those were awfully cute moments, but even cuter was when he said "Love?" and scratched the back of his neck, indicating that he would appreciate one of us scratching him there. After the boys started warming up to each other and Boston began following Fred around, perhaps seeing in him a powerful ally against bullying big brother Phoenix, Boston too began to say "Love?"

In terms of a captive macaw's lifespan, Fred was barely middle-aged, yet he'd still spent a quarter of a century in cage. It was big as cages go but still a cage. Our aviary was not a cage but a room, a big one, and there was none of this food-in-a-cup business. Nuggets, vegetables, and nut treats were hidden in tubes or wheels or wire contraptions from which they had to be shaken or pried. If the birds wanted to eat, they had to forage. This wasn't a cruel tease—just the opposite, in fact, since foraging was what they'd have to do in the wild and what macaws are very, very good at, so long as they're used to doing it. Fred wasn't used to it yet. Because Fred couldn't fly and needed to build up his climbing skills, Ken rearranged the various perches in the aviary to be more Fred-friendly, with more obvious and direct paths from one area to the next. Still, in the beginning he tended to stay in just one area, pulling on some of the foragers to make them swing back and forth but not yet manipulating the pellets from them. It was a brave new world for him.

Then there was the even stranger world known as outside. The first time we set Fred on an outdoor perch, he seemed stunned. What happened to the walls? Where's the ceiling? My god, what is that thing that looks like a gigantic piece of broccoli? A "tree," you say? Whoa! Everything seemed to fascinate him: butterflies, airplane contrails, twirling windblown corn husks, the elaborate bird fountain Ken had constructed from PVC pipes for the boys to splash around in on hot days. Perhaps I'm also guilty of anthropomorphizing, but there's something poignant about that kind of wary wonder. Discovering something new later in life can be terrifying or exhilarating, and usually both. I can relate.

But I related to another aspect of Fred's new life that wasn't quite so exuberant—was, in fact, sad. Fred's wing feathers had been clipped when he was very young, so he never learned to fly. He wasn't kept shut up in his cage, though, as his people allowed him to roam freely around the house. Feather clipping is common practice, and feather-clipped birds like Fred could still enjoy good lives with caring people. And yet ... they're birds. Keeping a bird from flying misses the point as much as keeping a horse in a stall all the time. And this is how we ended up with a dilapidated farmhouse on four acres of land in the middle of the cornfields. Our birds fly.

Well, at least Boston and Phoenix did. Fred was another story. Though his clipped wing feathers had long since grown back, flight seems to be something best learned at a very young age. Whenever Boston and Phoenix took off for a few loops around our property before landing high up in the giant broccoli, Fred stayed behind on his perch, alone. Sometimes we'd catch him fanning his wings awkwardly, frenetically, which could simply be a sign that he was anxious in these strange surroundings or could express an innate yearning to be up there too. Boston and Phoenix weren't flying aces yet— Boston in particular didn't always stick his landings, and while Phoenix was quite skilled at most aspects of flight, he hadn't used these skills in many places other than home. But Boston and Phoenix were only three years old; they had most of their lives ahead of them to explore the skies. Fred didn't and possibly never would.

Fred's limitations got me thinking a lot about my own, especially whenever I started or finished a long distance run. As mentioned, I've never believed anything is possible; many things are possible, sure, and because we don't always know what those things are, it behooves us to try a whole bunch of stuff. We might end up enthralled by and/or gloriously successful at some of them. But not even the most talented, privileged, fortunate person on earth can do whatever they want whenever they want it, especially since many endeavors have expiration dates. Fred may be too old to fly; someday, I may be too old to run as fast or as far as I want to—and, one day, too old to run at all.

No, I would remind myself daily as I laced up my Brooks, today is not that day. In fact, there are some plusses to getting older as a runner. Not many, but there's always Boston—the race, not the bird. It's kind of a big deal for marathoners, being one of the few in which nearly everyone who wants to run it must qualify by beating a certain age-graded time. For a fifty-year-old woman, the qualifying time is four hours. I am an OK runner but I've never considered myself all that fast, yet when I saw that four-hour qualifying time, an annoying little voice in my head whispered I think I can do that. I need to figure out how to shut that voice off.

Flight for our birds had always seemed similar to running for me: the surest, purest way to feel utterly alive. Ever since we'd gotten Boston and Phoenix, I'd secretly thought about the potentially magnificent symbolism in their names as relevant to my running. The mythical Phoenix rose from the ashes, but Boston was the one I had really hoped would rise. He had been a runt, slow to develop, but I wanted very badly for him to prevail. Picture it: The little blue-and-gold parrot named Boston who started so far behind ends up smart, strong, and utterly magnificent. The Boston Marathon is bombed and becomes more popular than ever. The runty high school girl who failed all those stupid Presidential Fitness Tests ends up running a Boston-qualifying marathon. Yes!

Well, the first two were yesses. Not so much the last. That isn't unusual; one of the fastest runners I know tried a good half dozen times before he got in. At the point where Fred had come to us, I had tried and failed three times. The most recent failure had been particularly hard to take. Training had been going well and, just as important for me, I was having fun. And then yet another running injury derailed everything, and I started to wonder how far off that day was, the day when I couldn't run anymore. Yes, age is just a number, and I didn't think my particular number was all that enormous (despite the fact that rotary-dial phones, rabbit-eared TVs, and even a manual typewriter figured prominently in my childhood). But there's a reason they make BQ times slower for older runners: many things get tougher with time, including running, flying, and fixing up an old house in the countryside.

I'd always been one to try new things, redefine myself, adapt to new situations, but now I wondered if there was a limit to how far I could go. Rarely a day went by when my husband and I didn't feel like we were in over our heads with this disastrous junk heap of a home. At the age when many people were reaching the peak of their working lives and beginning to look ahead at retirement, we were trying to do all this. I was pushing fifty and Ken had pushed past it. We may have been runners, but our bodies had limits. We were tired a lot—and discouraged when we failed.

There's a photo of me and Fred standing in the middle of our field on a windy day. Ken took it, in a moment when Boston and Phoenix were off flying together. Bird faces may be hard to read, but as I said on the first page of this book, body language—even, in this case, when the body has beautiful but not entirely useful wings—reveals a lot. The way Fred is looking up at me, leaning toward me—maybe it's wishful thinking, but I see something there very much like consolation, both given and received.

CHAPTER 16

Ridiculous Lengths

I DID MOST OF THE cooking for our household, mostly because I liked to cook and Ken often got home quite late in the evening (there was always a last-minute ferret mishap or chinchilla emergency), but Ken could hold his own in the kitchen just fine. Our cooking styles were similar—throw a bunch of stuff in a pan, add some sort of flavoring elements, throw it all on rice or pasta or tortillas and race each other eating it. I say I like to cook, but the truth is I no longer made any of the more elaborate dishes in my repertoire, in part to save money but mainly because spending hours on something that would be consumed in minutes no longer seemed sensible. This worked for both of us, since we weren't terribly fussy about our food.

I should say, we were not fussy about our *own* food. Matters were quite different when it came to feeding the parrots.

Ken's phone was permanently set for a 5:30 a.m. alarm, even when he wasn't running in the morning or didn't have an early meeting to attend. He needed the time to prepare the birds' breakfast. It was a very involved process—ridiculously involved. Sometimes when I was actually conscious at 5:30 a.m. I'd go downstairs to watch him work. It was a bit like watching a skilled and meticulous sous chef for an upscale vegan restaurant. As mentioned, one does not simply give macaws food. They have to work for it, so their people have to work too. Besides regular pellet food, the birds got a wide range of vegetables in the morning, all of which required unique preparation. Colorful grape tomatoes were arranged in special little cages; carrots and sweet potatoes were lightly microwaved and placed in wire spiral contraptions; corn cobs were cut into manageable chunks and strung on a kebab skewer along with pomegranate quarters and mini bell peppers. If the chunk of cob was an end piece with a bit of stem, Ken would tie a bit of sisal rope to the stem, like a sort of rustic pioneer's Christmas tree ornament. Boston in particular loved his corn; he'd take a wheel of it and systematically pick off one kernel at a time, 'round and 'round.

And that was just breakfast. As mentioned, the birds got regular pellet food, which required some labor as well. There were some eighty or ninety different foragers in their habitat, many fashioned out of inexpensive materials by Ken himself, given that the fancy shmancy foragers we'd gotten from stores were less durable than their packaging claimed— and given that the packaging often worked far better than the item itself. For a while we had been putting the pellets directly into foragers, but pretty soon that ceased to be enough of a challenge. Our boys extracted morsels as fast as we dispensed them. At that point Ken added another layer of challenge by wrapping the pellets in paper before stuffing them in the foragers. Our typical evening routine now involved eating our own dinner as fast as we could and then sitting with a tub of bird pellets and a pile of junk mail which we tore into squares and twisted around the pellets, one after another after another. No, Capital One, I'm not interested in your credit card offer, but thanks for the colorful envelope and inserts; they'll work nicely wrapped around a nut treat and stuffed in a PVC pipe.

Why go through all this trouble? Sometimes I wasn't sure. It was a little crazy, what we did for them, and I'll further admit that there are times I wondered: *is it worth it?* Even pets who aren't quite so high maintenance as macaws have a similar effect on their people. Anyone with a dog has likely left a party early out of concern for their canine's bladder relief. Even cats, for all their general aloofness, have needs to be met. Our turtles went into hibernation in late autumn, burying deep into the earth, after which we would not see them again until April, but we'd still know they were out there, and that still required us to be mindful of their welfare. Looking around me, I couldn't say that we'd *completely* organized our lives around our animals, but we mostly had, and most of that "mostly" was for Phoenix, Boston, and Fred. We lived here because of them. We planned vacations around them. Ken's daily routine, everything from the time he got up in the morning to the first place he headed—the avi-

ary—when he got home from work, was all about
them.

I understood all that. I was not a wife who insisted on being top priority. I was not even used to
being a wife. It was a relatively new thing for me to
be this much a part of anyone's life, so I could take
care of myself just fine when he needed to be elsewhere. Animals, kids, job, all had rightful demands
on his time. Our pets' lives literally depended on his
care. Children need their father. His job was massively stressful, unlike mine; he kept long hours,
and I understood that after a day of meetings,
teaching, consultations, surgeries, and other mis-
cellaneous duties that might well include inform-
ing someone that their beloved family member had
not made it, he might not want to come home and
start plastering walls or cutting tiles. I understood,
but that didn't make it any easier to live day after
day in a house whose decorating style appeared to
be post-apocalyptic.

The funny thing is I was able to put up with the
squalor reasonably well. We'd done this thing, and
we were here; what else was there but to accept it,
warts and all? More than accept it—laugh at it. It
struck me as comical when things kept going wrong.

It did not strike Ken any such way. "Worst decision ever," he said, again and again. "This place is a shithole."

"Sure it is, but it's *our* shithole!"

"I'm glad you like it because we don't have any money to fix it."

"We don't have to fix everything at the same time. It'll get done. It's a work in progress."

"All work and no progress."

"Since when am *I* the optimist here?"

He laughed, but he also acknowledged the truth in my words. I was being unaccountably positive, something neither of us was used to.

Part of my attitude adjustment was because I knew the squalor of the house was equally my fault. I had the time, but once Ken started losing interest in working on the house, I lost it too. Working by myself all day on something I wasn't very good at and didn't seem to be getting any better at started to seem like being punished for something I didn't do. I wasn't the one who got us here, after all, but I knew complaining about it, as enjoyable as that might be, would only make things worse. We were here, and we would remain here for a while, and the only way we could ever get *out* of here was by fixing up the place sufficiently so that we could resell it someday. And Ken was already thinking about re-selling it.

"Look at this. Forty acres for ten grand!"

Pause. Me, in a carefully neutral tone: "Where?"

"New Mexico. Look at the land. Wide open. Great views. Ten thousand dollars!"

Less neutral now. "Why's the price so low? What's wrong with it?"

"Nothing's wrong with it. There's nothing *there* to be wrong with it. It's just land, no running water, no power, no buildings."

"Wouldn't it be expensive to add all that stuff?"

"Actually, I've done some calculations..."

I listened, or at least put on the appearance of listening. In truth I was probably marveling at the déjà vu.

"Just look at the views!" He adjusted the laptop so we could both stare at the screen. "I would move there *now* if we could."

I said nothing, because I would not move there now, pretty sure I didn't want to move there ever. Yes, the views, but what were we supposed to *do* there? I am a solid introvert; interaction with people takes inordinate amounts of energy, even when those interactions end up being enjoyable. But I did not want to be a complete recluse. It was healthy to be around people at least once in a while. Plus, the practical side of me asserted, it was sensible. We weren't kids. If anything went wrong—because something always goes wrong—we'd be on our own. We would know not one single person in the entire state, nor in the states surrounding the entire state.

What's more, Ken might be perfectly contented to fly his birds all day, but I wouldn't be. We had already moved once because of them; we already had to plan our schedules around them. I wasn't about to let go of everything else because of them. Birds were still very much *his* thing, which meant that the things that were ours seemed to recede far away. His lack of interest in running these days was especially crushing to me. Running had brought us together, had been an activity we enjoyed in each other's company; now, to him, it was just yet another irksome demand on his time.

I knew what needed to happen. Instead of dreaming about escaping to the desert, we needed to do what we did a year ago: take a significant amount of time off to work on the house together. It wouldn't quite be a staycation since we'd be tackling projects, but it had to be done. We'd progressed so little since we'd purchased the house that I not-quite-kidded my friends who'd seen the place that they could only ever see it once in their lives, because if they ever came back, they'd realize how little we'd done. That needed to be a joke, not a reality. We had to do this, had to make our lives better here and now.

Instead, we packed up the truck and headed south.

CHAPTER 17

The Big Trip

Part 1

E ARLY IN OUR TRAVELS to the southwest, we spent a night in the parking lot of a gas station convenience store in Hinton, Oklahoma. This was not a planned stop, so don't bother Googling Hinton to see if it's got some amazing place for tacos or the childhood home of someone famous who got the hell out of there as fast as they could. As far as I know, Hinton has none of that, though it is the nearest town to Red Rock Canyon State Park, where we had stopped briefly to stretch our legs (and our wings, in the case of our macaws). It was a weekday, so the park was nearly empty, though our birds did make quite an impression on the handful of people we saw there, including a young couple in prim, formal clothing that suggested they might be Amish, who stopped to watch Phoenix descend gracefully down from a tree to Ken's arm. They smiled with delight. This happened a lot, not always with Amish people, but always with our birds, because even though everyone has an idea of what a parrot is, surprisingly few people have ever seen one up close and personal. One week, three states, and hundreds of miles later, at least a few more people can say they have.

We'd stopped at the Hinton convenience store after the park because we needed a roadmap. That's right, a good old-fashioned paper map to unfurl awkwardly and try to refold even more awkwardly so that it's a little less cumbersome to read. This was not out of nostalgia. Ken's phone was dying and the DC converter wasn't working and he had brought the wrong charger for the inverter (and I have no idea what I just said, as electronics are not my area of expertise at all). We had to go retro to get ourselves to New Mexico, where we intended to camp, hike, and fly our birds in as secluded a spot as we could find. The tricky part, or so we thought, would be the finding. When Ken came out of the store empty-handed and tried to start our moving-truck-turned-camper, we realized that the even trickier part would be avoiding spending our entire vacation in Hinton.

The truck had had a number of mechanical issues in the past, all of them loud and smelly. Parts screeched. Smoke wafted from the engine. Yet the most frustrating indicator of something gone terribly wrong was—nothing. When Ken turned the key in the ignition, nothing happened. No sound, no smoke, just silence and stillness. It was 4:30 p.m. on a Friday and we had no real idea where we were, other than that it wasn't where we wanted to be.

Ken walked up the street to an auto dealership and luckily found a couple of mechanics. They were jovial, jokey, chain-smoking guys who didn't seem at all put-out that we'd caught them right before quitting time. They checked the truck out. "The starter," they said, and one of them drove to the next town forty-five minutes away to get a new one. An hour and a half, a new starter, and $300 for parts and labor later, still nothing. They shrugged. They told us they'd left a message for their boss, who would get back to us tomorrow morning to see what he could do.

Of all the terrible things that can happen to a person, being stuck in a truck in a small town can't be considered more than a minor irritation. At the time, however, it felt a great deal worse than that. We'd been hankering to see the southwest for over a year, since we'd had to postpone this trip when we bought our old farmhouse. Back then we'd figured the time would be better spent on fixer-upper work than gallivanting around the desert. A year later, the farmhouse remained a fixer-upper, we had yet to gallivant, and we might be spending the whole weekend *here,* possibly much of the week if the truck needed some special parts that were a lot more than forty-five minutes away. We couldn't stay in a hotel, if Hinton even had one, because of our birds, and the manager of the gas station didn't seem terribly pleased that we'd be spending the night in their parking lot. I suppose it might have been different if our truck were a normal-looking camper, tan with brown swirls instead of white with white blobs where we'd painted over old graffiti. I suppose it might also have been different if we were from around there, which we clearly weren't, or if we otherwise fit in some easily relatable or grasp-able category, which we didn't. We'd sought escape in the vastness of the desert and instead we were crammed into 200 square feet with three restless birds and the suspicious eyes of small-town Okla-homa upon us. What were we *doing* here? What were we *thinking*? That question quickly became an accusatory, resentful *what were you thinking?* in each of our respective heads as our nerves frayed and our hopes of being able to salvage the week dwindled. We had been driving a long time. We were dirty and tired. If we ever got the truck moving again, it might be too late for us to do anything but turn back around and go home to our miserable old farm-house and wonder how two people could fail at so many things at once.

The next morning, Ken went back up the street to the dealership to see if the boss was in yet. A few minutes after he'd gone, I heard someone knocking on a window in the cab of the truck. A displeased-looking woman was peering suspiciously into the truck. "Nobody is supposed to park here overnight. Did you break down?" she asked. She was prob-ably the morning shift for the convenience store and the night shift had forgotten to let her know we'd be there, like they'd said they would. Yes, I told her, our truck broke down, we were here overnight—wasn't *that* fun!—and her manager was supposed to have been told. "Well, no one told *me*," she frowned.

I apologized like mad, explained our unique situation, how we couldn't go to a hotel because of our macaws. "What's that?" she asked, frowning again. Parrots, I explained, instantly realizing this wasn't going to make us seem any less like nutjobs. I kept apologizing and she seemed to relax a bit. "It's OK, I understand, but you know, I came in this morning and saw this unmarked truck here and, well," she leaned in and lowered her voice, "you know how things are these days." I nodded. I did, though I suspected my perspective on *these days* was likely very different from hers. There's an ugly, snobby side of me that threatens to take over in times like this, when I start to think about how little I have in common with the people around me, when I become hyper aware that I don't look like them or do the kinds of things they do. Yet, because I did the things *I* did, I was there.

Ken returned and the boss mechanic soon followed, along with the boss mechanic's son. The boy was maybe only nine or ten and looked a great deal like Bobby from *King of the Hill*. He was a little shy around us but competently assisted his dad, bringing various tools as requested. "They may be at it a while," Ken said to me grimly. "How are the boys?" They were restless, rattling their beaks against the cage walls like prisoners with tin cups. Ken shook his head. "I don't blame them. Let's take them out for some air."

I did not like this idea at all; we hardly needed to attract *more* attention to ourselves. Plus, all we'd need was for Boston to get up in a tree and camp out there for a while, as he was wont to do, while we cajoled and coaxed and begged him to come down, as hours went by, to make this experience *truly* special. But Ken had a point. We had not enjoyed being confined to a small space for a long time ourselves, and our birds were not normally kept in small cages; their habitat at home was so big we could have parked the entire truck within it. If this experience was frustrating for us, it was likely even more so for them. Out they came.

And out came everyone else. The woman I'd talked to earlier reemerged from the store wide-eyed and mouth agape, then ran back in to grab her phone for a photo. A young couple who had just pulled in to the parking lot in a car that was more wreck than car (and yet the engine *was* running, which was one up on us) got out and walked right over to us, as though we and not cigarettes were why they'd stopped. The Bobby look-alike was transfixed. Ken gave him a piece of walnut and instructed the boy how to hold the treat so that Fred would have to stretch a little to take it, which the big red bird did, gently and gratefully. The traveling parrot show was suddenly the hit of the town.

"I've never seen one before, only on TV," the boy said excitedly. "I want to get one someday."

Macaws were pretty much the reason we'd spent the night at the gas station, the reason we were traveling in a rickety moving truck instead of a car or a plane, the reason we couldn't stay at hotels or camp any place where their raucousness might disturb other people or visit anywhere that didn't allow pets. They were largely the reason the place we called home was a town far smaller and more depressing than this one and a house that barely qualified as having indoor plumbing. In short I was not feeling especially fond of our critters at the moment, but I do have at least a little bit of a heart, and seeing the kid's beaming face, all I said was, "They're a lot of work, though they can be a lot of fun too."

And then the truck engine suddenly roared back to life. As it turned out, the problem was a fuse—that's right, a cheap, postage-stamp-sized piece of equipment (so cheap and such an easy fix that the guy refused to charge us) had brought everything to a screeching halt. The boss mechanic had smartly taken an existing fuse from the truck—one for the blower, which we knew worked—and moved it to the starter to see if that was the problem. It was.

For want of a fuse the kingdom was very nearly lost, but now we could get on our way. The question was, which way. This time a fuse; what would it be next? The truck had been one minor disaster after another (full disclosure: this was not the first time we'd spent the night at a gas station parking lot, and I can tell you that these would be two times more than anyone who isn't a trucker getting paid for it needs to spend in a gas station parking lot). As bad as the night was, it could easily have been so much worse. The gas station had a restroom, at least, and all the junk food one could want. If we stalled in the middle of the desert, no one around for miles, which had sounded so appealing when we planned this trip and so very problematic now, what would we do? Did it really make sense to keep going?

You know full well we kept going.

I have never believed in simplistic solutions to complicated problems, so I can't be completely satisfied in gushing about how wonderful it was to spread some joy and bring different people together through our birds. We'd gone on this trip in part to escape humanity for a while, so bringing people together was not at all on our agenda. But humanity will never be escaped for long; we always come back to it, by plan or by accident, in the small spaces we inhabit in the brief time we're here.

Part 2

ONE OF THE MAIN reasons Ken and I went on this slightly crazy journey to the southwest with our birds was to fly them in the vast, open spaces of New Mexico. Where we live in rural Illinois is vast and open, too, but it's a privately owned vast-and-open, and a person can't exactly wander into some random field to launch a couple of macaws, not that many persons besides us are ever tempted to do this. New Mexico is checkerboarded with Bureau of Land Management parcels, much of which is open to the public for recreational use, and the terrain is perfect for our particular form of recreation: not many trees, good sight lines, starkly beautiful. To the desert we went.

After a quick stop at the Carlsbad BLM office to pick up a map (and to ask for suggestions on the best areas to fly birds, which the helpful BLM officer gave after only a brief pause of surprise), we headed out in search of the vastness. We found the suggested area fairly easily and pulled off the paved road into the parking area. I say "parking area" because there was a letter P on the map indicating that we could park there, but really this was no more than a slightly wider part of the dirt-and-gravel path. Because the path beyond there looked heavily cratered and the camper often has trouble on-road, much less off, we pulled over and stopped.

This particular patch of land was fairly close to town and featured jogging trails, so it wasn't nearly as remote as we had originally wanted. And though it was a weekday and we clearly would have the place all to ourselves, there were immediate—and disturbing—signs that other recreational activities had occurred here in the recent past. Next to the truck was a huge pile of garbage, or at least what looked cursorily like it: a filthy rolled-up carpet, a used condom, empty soda bottles, torn packaging for cookies, candy, and chips. On second glance, there was an eerie sort of order to the pile, suggesting that it had not merely been dumped and abandoned but *stored* there, on purpose. A little further up the path, Ken spotted the carcass of a coyote and the severed head of a deer amidst the scrubby bushes, along with a large blue water carboy. Again, the juxtaposition looked purposeful. This is the point in the movie where everyone in the audience is screaming "GET THE HELL OUT OF THERE YOU FOOLS." I was kind of screaming that in my head myself. We didn't, though; we'd come many hundreds of miles for the privilege of wondering what we'd gotten ourselves into, so we kept ourselves into it.

Ken took Boston and Phoenix, whom he launched immediately. I got Fred. Fred and the boys were getting along reasonably well, but there was far more wariness than chumminess between them, and we were a little concerned that instead of becoming the Three Amigos, they might forever remain the two that fly and the one that doesn't.

But a funny thing would happen when Boston and Phoenix took off: Fred noticed, very keenly, and reacted. First he would start squawking, loudly, with an edge of panic, as he watched them go, and then he would lean forward into the wind and flap his wings as hard as he could. When he started flapping his wings that particular morning, I stretched my arm out to give him more wingspan space and began to move. Fred flapped. I walked. We were flying together, sort of.

If Fred had never come to us, he would never have seen two other birds that look like him who could leap into the air and stay there, soaring, swooping, gliding, *flying*. Since he did, it's hard not to believe that something awakened in him, some realization of what he should have been able to do but couldn't, what he should *be* but wasn't, not completely. I wonder if we did him any favors. This was not a child on a bicycle which I would have to let go of. His claws digging into my bare arm hurt, but he had to hold on to me and I had to stay with him. Though when the wind caught his wings just right, I could feel him lift just a little. It wasn't enough.

As you thoroughly know by now, my relationship with our birds has been difficult. They are high-maintenance pets, certainly, but all pets are if you do it right, and that wasn't the difficult part. I was having a hard time figuring out what these three animals were supposed to mean to me, and I to them. I helped care for them, but Ken did most of the work there, and they knew it—every creature who wants to survive figures out quickly where its next meal is likely to come from. I admired their beauty and chuckled at some of their antics (Fred had this trick where he picked up a stick in his claw, waved it up and down like a symphony conductor, and then pretended to scratch the back of his head with it), but everyone who saw them could admire them in that way. I was still anywhere from mildly to violently afraid of being bitten, mainly by Phoenix, who was the best at both flying and breaking things. I certainly did not wish them any harm, because it's hard to witness any living creature being harmed regardless of what they might mean to you personally.

And the truth is I did not know what they meant to me personally. I had loved Cayenne, but the birds were like tropical fish to me—beautiful and remote. I could admire them and see to their welfare, yet so far there had been no deeper attachment. I did not understand them, and I could not see anything recognizable in them at all.

Until now. When Fred perched on my arm trying to fly, there it was, understanding and recognition.

It wasn't until a couple of days later that I realized something more. We had reached south Texas after driving for several hours through an indescribably ugly area of oil rigs, when suddenly all of that ended and we were in a beautiful land again, mountains and valleys and even some color despite its being mid-December. Spotting a rest stop off the road, we pulled over to once again stretch our legs and wings.

It was windy again, but much colder; a storm was coming in following a freakish heatwave, and Fred's claws this time sank into a thick coat sleeve instead of my bare flesh. All three of the boys like windy days. Phoenix and Boston love to go zooming by with the wind at their backs, turning sharply and then floating gracefully back down to Ken's arm. Even Fred seems more willing to faux-fly in the wind. But not this day. The wind had teeth, and instead of leaning into it and spreading his wings, Fred fluffed up and huddled close to me. While Ken worked with Boston and Phoenix, Fred and I wandered slowly around the rest stop, watching them. At that point I looked down at the big red bird sitting quietly on my arm. He looked back up at me, and I felt it: love.

There are wrong reasons to love something. Ideally, at its best, we love a thing not because of what it does for us but because of what it is and what our love can do for it. But let's be honest, most love is at least a little, and often a lot, selfish. I fell in love with my husband because he was exactly what I wanted and needed. Yes, I also fell in love with him because he's a good person, but Jimmy Carter is a good person and I'm not sending *him* so much as a Christmas card. At that moment I knew I loved Fred because I was with him while he experienced one of the saddest emotions of all, one that doesn't even have a proper name (at least not in English, though I'm sure the Germans have one). It's not quite regret— you can't regret something that could never happen in the first place—so much as impossible yearning. I loved him because he looked so calm and peaceful there on my arm, but also so vulnerable. And I loved that these were all things I recognized, potently, in myself.

At that point Phoenix suddenly swooped toward us, so I held up my other arm for him to land. This had happened a few times over the past week, Phoenix and Boston each deciding to come to me instead of Ken, and while it surprised the heck out of me, we took it as a sign that they were including me in their world, that they trusted me and maybe even liked me. I looked down at the two birds on my arms, one I loved, and the other ... well ... "I'm working on it," I murmured to Phoenix. That seemed to appease him, so he turned and flew back toward Ken, up into the wind and then down, all radiant color yet full of mystery, descending like an angel.

Part 3

LET'S BACK UP A bit.

As nice as it was to spend time with my new buddy Fred, we had gone on this trip in large part to fly Boston and Phoenix—far away from home, for the first time. At the BLM land near Carlsbad, the place with the garbage pile and the severed deer head, we finally got a chance to do that.

After we parked the truck, we walked about a mile down a rough dirt road until we came to an open area that seemed like a good place to launch

Boston and Phoenix. Ken realized he'd left his bird bag back at the truck, and with it all the indispensable tools for dealing with the boys, including treats, target stick, and clickers (which are used to signal to the bird that he has done something good and a reward is coming). I volunteered to go back, at which point Ken suggested I just drive the whole truck out here, so we'd have everything. I cringed a little at the idea of navigating around all those crater-like potholes and jagged boulders in a big, ungainly vehicle with a couple of axles just begging to be broken. Still I agreed and ran the mile back to the parking lot.

I drove about as slowly as a person can drive a motor vehicle without going backwards, and somehow I made it back to Ken without tipping over. Triumphant, I got out and handed the keys to Ken, who stood alone with Fred.

"They're gone."

I blinked a few times. "What do you mean, gone."

"I can't find them."

More blinks. "What do you mean—"

"*I don't know where they are.*"

I looked around at the wide open emptiness. How the hell could they have just vanished?

"Where did they—I mean, what direction were they headed?"

He pointed back the way I had come. "Off that way. I think they were following *you*. Maybe they wanted to see where you were going."

I stared back down the road. So we had finally realized the dream of flying our birds while running, and naturally it had not gone as planned.

We got back in the truck and now Ken was the one who had to negotiate the crazy dirt road. He's a far more confident driver than I am and took it at a more forthright speed, which only added to my certainty that we would compound the disaster of losing the boys in the desert with tipping over in the truck and getting out alive only to be hacked to death by whoever who collected animal carcasses out here.

Back out on the paved road, Ken pointed to a small cluster of trees, pretty much the only trees in the vicinity. "I think they went this way. It makes sense that they'd be here."

None of this made *sense*, I wanted to snap. Driving over a thousand miles in an old moving truck to let a couple of macaws fly in the desert is not a scenario that would make anyone think, "Oh, sensible!" Standing in a ditch on the side of the road yelling *Boston! Phoenix!* over and over is not an activity that makes a person appear to have any sense at all. But there we were.

"Boston! Phoenix!"

And then, as if we were at home and they'd just done a spin around the field, a flash of bright red burst from the trees followed by another flash of mixed blue and yellow as Phoenix and Boston flew straight to Ken. "Good boys!" he exclaimed happily.

A few minutes before this, those good boys were giving us each several heart attacks apiece. Now they were safely back in their cage and Ken was feeling pleased. But even he knew better than to push his luck. He decided to call it a day. I did not have a problem with that. I was glad that their brief disappearance had turned out to be a non-event, but I dreaded future free-flights.

Fast forward to Texas, in an RV park outside of Big Bend. We were the only ones in the entire place, and even the National Park itself seemed all but deserted. A big snowstorm was supposed to hit in two days and all of southwest Texas was freaking out, given that any snow at all in this part of the world can be considered a big snowstorm. We were delighted to be the only campers in our park, pleased with the privacy and relieved that no one would be bothered by our noisy entourage. After another long day of driving, Ken decided to let the entourage out.

Ken and I still occasionally joked about Phoenix's crow nemesis way back at Level 1. For all that he liked to bully Boston around, Phoenix was hardly invulnerable and had been reduced to a quivering mass of scarlet feathers by a smaller bird. It amused us now because no harm had come to anyone. It did not seem quite so amusing when, seemingly out of nowhere, two large crows materialized as soon as we launched the boys at the RV park.

The terrain of this area was different from where we'd flown them in New Mexico. Southwest Texas definitely looks southwestern, with wide open plains of low, scrubby plants, but it also has mountains, big ones. That combination creates a powerful trompe l'oeil landscape in which it can be difficult to judge distance and proximity. The moment the crows began to follow Boston and Phoenix, the boys took off straight away from us toward the looming mountains to the south, flying fast. I wouldn't even say the crows were chasing them—it looked more like curiosity than aggression—but the boys, led as always by Phoenix, were having none of that.

Eventually the crows moved on, perhaps bored with the game. Boston and Phoenix kept going. Even though they were no longer being chased, they flew arrow-straight away from us, toward the mountains, which suddenly seemed a lot closer and higher and more easily reachable by a couple of birds—but not a couple of people. When were they going to start arcing to come back? It was like watching the Titanic swerving to avoid the iceberg, and we all know how that turned out. I hadn't realized at the time that Ken was recording the flight on his phone. We never posted the video. The only thing you can hear is Ken yelling their names and me muttering "Oh shit oh shit oh shit" as I watched them recede.

They were at least a mile away. If they stopped and landed now we would never be able to get close enough to call them back and we would never see them again. They'd never been here before; they'd never be able to find their way back.

Come back.

Come BACK.

Were they coming back? Were they veering off just a little? I couldn't tell.

My agitation was starting to agitate Fred, who I'd almost forgotten was still on my arm. I decided to put him back in the truck while Ken kept his eyes trained on the colorful specks in the distance. I spent a while fussing with Fred's cage, straightening the newspaper at the bottom, giving him treats, listening to him say "Hi?" and "Love?" I did not want to go out and hear Ken say once again, *They're gone*, because this time it would be permanent. This was our Level 5, where you had to trust your birds completely. I had never trusted them completely. There wasn't much in the world I trusted at all. It wasn't their fault; I didn't trust them only because I had limited control over them. We lost control of Cayenne that one afternoon and she slipped away from us forever. Now here we were, helpless in the face of another potential loss. This is how life goes, I know. I just wished it didn't have to go that way at that particular moment.

I steeled myself and went outside again. Ken stood there, still alone, arms raised, making the hand-waving gesture that meant *come here*.

I met his eyes.

And then the birds returned.

They landed quietly, each to an arm, Boston first and then Phoenix. It had easily been the longest time in the air either of them had experienced, yet they were back as though it had been just another trip around the block. "Good boys!" Ken shouted, a swell of joy in his voice.

From inside the truck, Fred called, "Love?"

CHAPTER 18

Return

THAT WASN'T THE END of the trip, obviously. We went hiking in Big Bend, then had to cut the trip short because of the snowstorm, then made the long drive back. It was roughly the same number of miles we'd driven to get out here, but the situation was drastically different now. First off, Ken wanted to drive straight through the night without stopping so we could get home as soon as possible. Second, it was a good fifty degrees colder than when we'd first set off.

Remember back when we were in Hinton? How the mechanic took the fuse from the blower and put it in the starter? This meant we were one fuse short and could not operate the blower—which meant we could not get any heat. This had not been a problem when the temperatures were mild. They were anything but mild on the drive back. It was nighttime, too, so we couldn't stop at a store to buy a fuse. Worse, the truck's wonky diesel engine did not work well—sometimes not at all—in the cold. If we stopped for the night at an RV park, we might be stuck there. And so we kept going.

I once ran a half marathon in Inverness, Scotland, in March. There had been an uncharacteristic snowstorm there, too, and although that part of Scotland is known for cold, damp weather, even the locals were saying this was a bad one. I had congratulated myself on securing a lovely hotel room with a view of the river just a mile from the start/finish. Well, I had never been so cold in my whole life as I trudged back to my room after the race: soaked to the skin, tired, bent into the wind, understanding why the Scots invented whisky. At the time it was the coldest I'd ever been. Now it's a distant second to that night we drove home.

Hour after hour after hour of relentless, biting cold. We were going to die, I was sure of it. *We are gonna freeze to death in an ugly old moving truck, I* thought. I looked back at Fred, all fluffed up on his perch, and then glared at Ken. *If Fred dies before we do, I will kill you. Eye for an eye, tooth for a beak.*

We didn't die. We finally made it back without losing any digits to frostbite, but we were incredibly cold, and tired, and dirty. I swear I haven't been that filthy since I came out of the womb. It was one of those times when all you want is a hot shower and a nap, and when I went to turn on the water for the first part of the equation, I got a thin icy trickle from the faucet because apparently forty-eight is too low to set the thermostat in the interest of saving on propane and our pipes were partially frozen.

"Uh, Ken? Remember when we first moved in and you said living here would be an adventure, like we were camping all the time?"

He gave me the look you give when you can't take one more thing going wrong but you know that's just what you're going to get.

We managed to get the water running eventually, but we continued to be cold, that day and the months that followed, a combination of record-low winter temperatures and the fact that some critter had chewed through all the heating ducts in the crawlspace. We considered moving in with the macaws, since their room was nice and toasty. Instead, Ken went down into the crawlspace to reattach the ducts, sliding through the narrow tunnels on a plastic toboggan with his night running headlamp and a surgical mask. It was horrible down there, which I say having only crouched near the opening of it. For Ken it was like leaping into an open grave and having a house fall on you. He persevered, however, and the ducts got fixed, but we couldn't even cross it off our to-do list because it hadn't been on the list in the first place. We had returned from our brief escape to find that, surprise! nothing had changed.

But to paraphrase that trite-but-true aphorism, be it ever so humble—and boy was our house that—there's one place called home that engenders feelings like no other, whether you're dying to get away from it or can't wait to return. We had made it back together, us and our macaws. That was something.

WHEN I SAT DOWN to write this book, I had all these separate anecdotes and episodes, but nothing in the way of an overarching theme. I liked overarching themes.

Ken said, "Well, that's easy. The theme is how these birds ruined our lives."

I was taken aback. Just like that, he'd figured it out.

But I knew it was more than that. Stories, as I've said, aren't just about what happens. They're about what *matters*. *Why* did they ruin our lives? How could this happen—how did we let this happen? And of course, as in most compelling stories, it didn't just happen, and we didn't merely "let" it happen. We caused it to happen. We went willingly to our ruin, and we burned all the bridges, boats, and maps that might give us a chance to say "just kidding" and go back the way we came. *Why?*

Runners love to talk about why they run, oblivious to the fact that nobody else cares, certainly not non-runners. When someone asks *why do you run those crazy distances?* they aren't really seeking an answer. Mostly I think they just want to make fun of you in an indirect way, so indirect that you won't even realize it. In any case, the answers runners give tend to be similar, many of them focused on the way running makes them feel truly alive, despite—sometimes because of—all the pain and suffering. I wondered if that was why we went through so many tribulations with our macaws. Did we feel more alive in the presence of these vibrant, vital creatures—or was that just a rationalization of all the things we put ourselves through?

Despite all we did put ourselves through, they didn't ruin our lives, not really. We're still here, as are they. In fact, the question could, and no doubt will, be asked if we didn't come closer to ruining *their* lives. Ken loves birds. He would never do anything he thought would cause them harm. But then all animal lovers are this way; they all want to do what's best for animals, and they all think they are doing just that. It's so much more convenient when it's simple, when there's a Michael Vick or Jimmy John we can demonize for their horrifying cruelty toward innocent creatures. I get it. I become fist-clenchingly enraged whenever I think about rhinoceroses being slaughtered because a lot of people still somehow believe that rhino horns have magical properties. The horns are keratin; you might as well chew off and swallow your own fingernails for all the magic you'll receive, and at least that way nothing will go extinct. But for every instance where humans are disgustingly, egregiously in the wrong in their treatment of other animals—

and there are plenty of these instances—there's another that's far murkier. Free-flight puts pet birds at greatly increased risk. Is this really best for the bird? On the one hand, it gives them a life that's closer to the life they were "meant" to lead, in the wild, but at the same time, they *aren't* in the wild. What purpose is served by believing that this risk is more for their sake than ours? Is even having them as pets more for our sake than theirs? It's true that animals in captivity often live longer than animals in their natural habitat, and it has even be argued that their quality of life is better in many ways. Who wants to spend their whole life running away from predators, trying to avoid being eaten while simultaneously struggling not to starve to death yourself? Most of the exotic animals kept in zoos or as pets in the U.S. were either born in captivity or else "rescue" animals, and, treated right, these animals need not merely be something to gawk at, a slave to human whim; they can live satisfying lives and even help educate people about conservation. The question is, what's the "right" way to treat them, and who has the right to decide?

Contentious questions. Not debatable at all, however, is the fact that we do coexist. It is impossible for humans not to have an effect on other animals. We can only keep trying to make this effect a positive one for all involved, and because that's never going to be simple, it's way beyond the scope of this one little book. At the same time, I do think there's a bigger picture here than that of two people and three birds on four acres in rural Illinois. These birds came into my life largely against my will. I didn't want them, and I didn't love them, not at first, yet there they were—here they are—and I had to learn how to live with them, just as I continued to learn how to live with the man who brought them into our lives. I guess this makes me a bird person after all.

The first question people ask when you say you have macaws is, "Do they talk?" We answer, *Not much, and that's just fine.* The first question people ask when you say you free fly your macaws is, "Don't they ever try to leave?" The answer: *No, they don't want to leave. They want to fly.* There are moments when you aren't thinking ahead or back but just enjoying what you're doing. That's how it was when Ken and I ran together, hearts beating, lungs pumping, blood flowing through our bodies, and I believe—I *know*—that's how it is for Boston and Phoenix when they streak through space, just as I know that's what Fred yearns for as he watches them. It's easy to see how they are simply enjoying the hell out of being alive in each other's presence, no matter what else happens during the rest of their time on earth. And this is why, even though the risks are undeniably enormous for all of us, free-flying our birds continues to be as much a part of my life, of *our* lives, Ken's and mine, as theirs—these beautiful, frustrating, linked-forever lives.

Afterword

AS THIS BOOK WAS getting ready to go to press, something unexpected happened.

It was a windy day in March. The winter had been a bad one and the boys were stir-crazy, so we let them out for the first time in a while. Windy days actually tend to make flight easier for Boston and Phoenix, since they can ease into their landings by simply floating down to Ken's arm against the breeze. Fred, watching the other two from an outdoor perch, spread his wings and flapped frenetically as usual. Then a gust of wind hit him, and the next thing he knew, he was airborne.

Gliding isn't flying, of course, but rather than simply being carried by the wind, Fred did what he'd tried to do all along in imitating the other two. And Fred flew. It was wobbly, and he landed unceremoniously on the ground after about a hundred yards, but it was *flight*, for the first time in his 27-year-old life.

That evening back in the aviary, Fred was quiet and wide-eyed. He seemed stunned by what had happened.

Frankly, we were too.

"This changes everything," Ken said to me.

To be continued...

Appendix

By Kenneth R. Welle, DVM, and Letitia L. Moffitt

You've just read about all the ways birds took over our lives, and you've somehow decided this is something you want for yourself. Congratulations! And, condolences. Here's some information to get you started.

Some clarification on the names

"Parrot" means birds of the order *Psittaciformes*. There are roughly 350 species within that order. The smallest is probably the parrotlet, about the size of a sparrow; the heaviest is the kakapo (a terrific name), which is about the size of a big chicken. The main thing that defines parrots is that they have a hooked beak that is very useful for crushing things like seeds and nuts as well as for climbing and other types of manipulation. No other types of birds use their beaks for locomotion. Parrots also have a thick, muscular tongue which no other bird has. The tongue also can manipulate and feel things—they use it like a finger (and, FYI, it is a very dry tongue—no doggie slobbering).

There are around fifty types of parrots that are commonly kept as pets, and maybe another fifty that are uncommonly kept as pets. No new birds are being imported into the U.S., so basically any pet parrot you get right now would be either an older bird or one that was bred in captivity. (This isn't necessarily the case in other countries, but in the U.S. a ban on importing parrots was created in 1992.)

"Macaws" are a group of South American parrots with just a few genera (a subdivision under family but above species). These all share a few basic characteristics. Many are large, like our boys, but there are some smaller ones that might be nearly a tenth the size of a green-wing like Phoenix.

If you just want a bird as a pet

BIG AND LOUD TENDS to be not so good, for obvious reasons. They're going to bother people with the noise and they require a lot more space. Keep in mind that many pet birds—large or small, noisy or quiet—have a life expectancy that's much longer than the more traditional dog-and-cat pets. Their requirements are not always easy to meet, both behaviorally and physically. It's worthwhile to do a lot of research to make sure you really want a bird at all, and then more to determine what type you want to bring home. Learn about the personalities of the different kinds of pet birds to see what works for you.

If you want to free-fly birds

BIG AND LOUD IS good. There are very few aerial predators large enough to go after a big bird like a green-wing macaw (though a gutsy crow might decide to chase one just for fun). A loud bird will be easy to track and locate—you can hear them long before you see them. Colorful birds are also a lot easier to spot in trees, on rooftops, etc. Big, loud, colorful birds includes macaws, cockatoos (many are white rather than colorful but they are still fairly easy to

spot), and some conures (smaller but faster-flying and agile). Really any bird can free-fly—pigeons are especially popular, for example—but the qualities listed here confer advantages in the event that a bird (inevitably) goes astray.

Different types of birds—and, of course, different individual birds—have different personalities. A bird needs to be very social with people—that is, it needs to want to be with people—as well as very attached to their person in order for free-flight to work. Importantly, a bird also needs to be a good flier to begin with. This may seem obvious, but surprisingly many people seem to believe the opposite is true: that a bird that doesn't fly very well is "safer" to fly because they can't get far away. As we witnessed with our Boston, it's more complicated than that. The easiest part of flight is getting up into the air. Far tougher is maneuvering, navigating, negotiating wind, and landing. A bird with poor flight skills, like Boston was in his early fledging days, can launch into the air but then have no idea what to do from that point and may get scared and tired and simply crash land into a tree—and not know how to get down. Birds with stronger flight skills will have an easier time getting back to their person.

Where to get birds

IF YOU WANT TO free-fly birds, this is a lot easier to do with a younger bird that is just fledging. They'll be the most receptive to learning the skills they need. That means going to a breeder. If you're just looking for a pet, there are a great many birds in rescues that need good homes. Some of these birds are going to be a lot less suitable for free-flight because of physical ailments or simply a lack of experience, but, as with our Fred, they can make great companions.

As for pet stores, there are great pet stores and poor pet stores, so it's best to assess an individual store to determine whether its animals will be healthy and well cared for.

Getting a bird at a bird convention or bird fair can be risky, as these birds are often highly stressed, which makes them vulnerable to infectious diseases.

Habitat creation

WHILE YOU MAY NOT want to or be able to move to the country and build an aviary, the truth is that

cages tend to be inadequate. A good habitat should be modeled less on the idea of a cage and more on an open room. Consider your bird's size and make sure there's enough space for the bird to move. Even if you aren't free-flying, the bird will still need some form of exercise, such as climbing and swinging. And if you do intend to free-fly, they'll need enough space for short indoor flights. You'll also need a lot of things for the bird or birds to chew and play with, and if the cage is too small, it will be overcrowded with all this *stuff*. You should also consider additional places for the bird to inhabit besides just their cage—open stands, for, example—so they aren't spending twenty-four hours a day in the same place.

Note that birds are social creatures, which means that you should seriously consider getting more than one. The birds don't have to be the same type of bird (though close in size is a good idea in general) and they don't need to stay in the same habitat as long as they can see each other.

Food and water

IN MANY CASES, HUMANS simply cannot replicate what birds eat in the wild. What wild macaws eat, for example, doesn't exist in the U.S. The best we can do is provide them with a nutritionally balanced diet, which is available in many pelleted foods. A variety of sizes for pelleted foods can be useful so that different types of foragers can get appropriate-sized nuggets. Pelleted food can also be supplemented with fresh vegetables. A little fruit is OK, but most fruits are largely sugar (particularly things like apples, bananas, and grapes, which tend to be what people give their pet birds), and too much sugar isn't good for anyone. Small amounts of fruits like melons, berries, or pomegranates are fine.

Other foods (pelleted and otherwise) can be used for training and enrichment purposes—for example, nuts and seeds. These should be limited in quantity; they're treats, rewards for good behavior, not staples.

Obviously birds need water. They can get it in a number of forms: dishes, sipper bottles (the ones often found in hamster and rabbit cages, with a

metal tube and ball at the bottom to dispense the water), or even regular water bottles used by runners. We found that water in dishes tends to get dirty quickly, especially since our boys would often drag food items through the water to make soup.

Enrichment

"ENRICHMENT" IS ANYTHING THAT improves the quality of life of the animal. One key component of enrichment is foraging.

Wild birds spend about half their awake time foraging for food. On the other hand, a pet bird who is given food in a dish will spend about 30 minutes "foraging." All that extra free time does not mean the bird can pick up a few fun hobbies. Instead, many birds pick up unhealthy displacement behaviors—that is, they replace a normal behavior with something that is often a harmful behavior, like feather picking or pacing. Because of this, it's healthier for a bird not just to eat but to forage.

The ultimate goal is to increase the amount of time the bird spends obtaining and consuming food. The way to do this is to provide the food in ways that create challenges. The tough thing is finding a balance, not making the challenge so hard that the bird quits or gets frustrated but hard enough that the bird does have to work for it.

Foragers should match the feeding style of the bird. A cockatiel or budgie normally feeds on the ground, so it makes sense to put foragers on the floor of their habitat, whereas hanging things make more sense for macaws since they normally feed in trees. Start with easy foragers and increase the complexity over time. The bird needs to build confidence, so don't start with the tough stuff right away. For example, for a bird that has never foraged before, you can start by putting food in many different dish feeders around the habitat, so they have to move around to feed. You can introduce safe "distractors" in with the food (such as rocks, shredded paper, or wooden beads) so that they have to pick through to find the pellets, and you can put a cover on the dishes that must be removed. From there you can gradually increase the challenges, all the way up to very complicated puzzle toys requiring intricate manipulation.

Health care

EVEN BEFORE YOU GET your bird, find and start a conversation with an avian veterinarian to make sure you can get appropriate care. When you first get your bird, bring them in for a visit. If you want your bird to free-fly, discuss this with your veterinarian (free-flying birds are at greater risk for certain infectious diseases, among other risks). Some vets will strongly encourage wing-clipping. There may be blood tests and such that the vet wants to perform to establish that you have a healthy bird. The vet can also help evaluate diet and other aspects of the animal's care, and a good one will also know about important behavior and training aspects

Training

ESSENTIALLY TRAINING AMOUNTS TO the following: 1) Trying either to catch a bird doing a behavior you want them to do or to "manipulate" them into doing it, and then reinforcing that behavior with some kind of treat or reward; 2) Later trying to connect a cue to that behavior so you can get the bird to perform the behavior when you want them to.

This may sound simple. It isn't, which is why we recommend taking classes. There are aspects to training, such as timing of the cue and reinforcement, that have to be applied at precisely the right time and sequence, and people also need to learn to read the bird's body language. There are both web-based and in-person classes to learn techniques to apply with your own bird.

Free-flight

NOT FOR THE FAINT of heart! Seriously, think long and hard about this before you decide to do it. That said, it's a great thing for the birds to do and a fun thing to experience yourself. There are a small number of professionals that offer specific training in free-flight (easily found via an online search), and if you're interested in free-flight, you should *not* begin without taking one of these courses.

Other pets and birds

FOR ALL THE CUTE YouTube videos of cute birds perched on kitties or puppies, this is extremely dangerous. Any veterinarian is likely to be able to tell you horror stories of birds killed by another pet. Do not carelessly allow contact between your bird and other animals, no matter how adorable it might be.

Final word

THE REWARD OF BEING able to see birds doing what they were meant to do is phenomenal. It is simply beyond compare. If this is something you want to undertake, good luck—and enjoy!

Resources

- Association of Avian Veterinarians (www.aav. org): Here you can find listings of avian vets and resources on pet bird care and health, as well as conservation-related information.

- Avian Behavior International (avian-behavior. org): Listings of workshops about bird behavior and free-flight programs.
- Good Bird Inc. (www.goodbirdinc.com): Good training resources.
- BahaviorWorks(www.behaviorworks.org): More good training resources.
- Libertywings (www.libertywings.com): Web-based training for free flight.

Photo Credits

About the Author

LETITIA L. MOFFITT WAS born and raised in Hawaii. She received a doctoral degree in English/Creative Writing from Binghamton University, and she taught creative writing at Eastern Illinois University for five years. She has written a novel-in-stories, *Sidewalk Dancing* (Atticus Books) and two paranormal mysteries *Trace* and *Vibe/Sync* (Cantraip Press). She and her husband, Ken Welle, live with their three macaws in rural Illinois. In her spare time, she runs marathons and ultramarathons

Made in the USA
Middletown, DE
29 July 2019